To Elder Ernest Young, my "big brother,"

mentor and teacher for his friendship and instruction

To servants of the King everywhere

waiting to emerge from their wilderness walks

Table of Contents

The Gospel of the Kingdom
Rediscovering the Core Message of Jesus and the Apostles

By

S. Lloyd Walters

Acknowledgement

Special thanks to Frank Runnels

for insights that helped initiate

this wonderful journey

The Gospel of the Kingdom

Rediscovering the Core Message of Jesus and the Apostles

by

S. Lloyd Walters

Preface

From the earliest recollections of my interest in ministry, one passion has dominated my motivation. It is what drove me to preach on street corners and debate the virtues of following Christ rather than Mohammed with young Muslims in Bedford-Styvesant, Brooklyn. It took me from city to city, preaching and teaching in churches, tents and storefronts.

Decades later, after college, seminary and doctoral studies, this same unrealized passion still burned within. Pastoring and proclaiming the Word was wonderful, but there was something else for which I hungered. One question remained unanswered after more than forty years of service to the King: Where is the power that the apostles walked with and why is it not as evident now?

There are certainly many who claim to operate in that anointing, and perhaps some do. Yet, healing leprosy (which was an incurable death sentence similar to AIDS or cancer today) as readily as Jesus did, to my knowledge, is not in evidence today. The power to heal and deliver every person in a town like the apostles and Phillip the deacon and evangelist did is not taking place.

This passion drove me to seek God and His Word for answers. Those answers did not come easily. There was a price to pay. The first question was, Would I be willing to pay that price? Once it was determined that there was nothing that would be placed before receiving this revelation, the Word began to come forth.

The revelation had been there all along. It had not been

taught in the setting that I had grown up and was subsequently trained in. In fact, it seemed as if operating without the power of God was preferred or had actually become the norm for many churches, ministries and denominations. Money and medicine were preferred over miracles.

What God revealed was that the message that John the Baptist, Jesus and the apostles taught and proclaimed was confirmed with signs, wonders and miracles. The Father also showed me that He would only visit those who had been tested and tried, and who were sharing the specific word that He wanted delivered with the confirmation of His power. Any deviation or corruption of this gospel would affect the extent of the manifestation of His power and presence. Even a little leaven would affect the whole lump, and the enemy would be sure to make every attempt to introduce multiple contaminants to this powerful message.

The message that they taught and proclaimed was the Gospel of the Kingdom. It was not a fad, slogan or a popular label that was tacked on as an afterthought on everything that they did. It was a specific and substantive word from the Father confirmed by the prophets of the Old Covenant and the apostles of New Covenant. It was the new wine that could not be contained by the old wineskins and the new fabric that could not be attached to the old cloth. Jesus said this Gospel (Good News) of the Kingdom must be preached in the whole world as a witness before the end comes.

It is a simple message, yet, apparently many missed it in Jesus' day and, it appears, in this day as well. I missed it in my years of training and subsequently my teaching of others. Now, having received this revelation, I am sharing, like one beggar among other hungry beggars, the bread that I have been freely given.

This discussion is, by no means, the last word on this subject. Hopefully, it will inspire and inform others who share my passion for service to the King and wish to operate in the fullness of His anointing.

The Gospel of the Kingdom

Rediscovering the Core Message of Jesus and the Apostles

Chapter 1

Introduction

1 Timothy 6:12-16

> Fight the good fight of the faith. Take hold of the eternal life
> to which you were called when you made your good confession
> in the presence of many witnesses. In the sight of God, who
> gives life to everything, and of Christ Jesus, who while testify-
> ing before Pontius Pilate made the good confession, I charge
> you to keep this command without spot or blame until the ap-
> pearing of our Lord Jesus Christ, which God will bring about
> in his own time—God, the blessed and only Ruler, the King of
> kings and Lord of lords, who alone is immortal and who lives
> in unapproachable light, whom no one has seen or can see. To
> him be honor and might forever. Amen.

2 Timothy 2:8-9

> Remember Jesus Christ, raised from the dead, descended from
> David. This is my gospel, for which I am suffering even to the
> point of being chained like a criminal. But God's word is not
> chained.

John 18:36-37

> Jesus said, "My kingdom is not of this world. If it were, my
> servants would fight to prevent my arrest by the Jews. But now
> my kingdom is from another place." "You are a king, then!"
> said Pilate. Jesus answered, "You are right in saying I am a king.

In fact, for this reason I was born, and for this I came into the world, to testify to the truth. Everyone on the side of truth listens to me."

Luke 1:31-33

You will be with child and give birth to a son, and you are to give him the name Jesus. He will be great and will be called the Son of the Most High. The Lord God will give him the throne of his father David, and he will reign over the house of Jacob forever; his kingdom will never end."

Matthew 2:2, 11, 4:23, 9:35, 10:5-7, 24:14

and asked, "Where is the one who has been born king of the Jews? We saw his star in the east and have come to worship him."

On coming to the house, they saw the child with his mother Mary, and they bowed down and worshiped him. Then they opened their treasures and presented him with gifts of gold and of incense and of myrrh.

Jesus went throughout Galilee, teaching in their synagogues, preaching the good news of the kingdom, and healing every disease and sickness among the people.

Jesus went through all the towns and villages, teaching in their synagogues, preaching the good news of the kingdom and healing every disease and sickness.

These twelve Jesus sent out with the following instructions: "Do not go among the Gentiles or enter any town of the Samaritans. Go rather to the lost sheep of Israel. As you go, preach this message: 'The kingdom of heaven is near.'

And this gospel of the kingdom will be preached in the whole world as a testimony to all nations, and then the end will come.

Acts 28:23; 30-31

> They arranged to meet Paul on a certain day, and came in even larger numbers to the place where he was staying. From morning till evening he explained and declared to them the kingdom of God and tried to convince them about Jesus from the Law of Moses and from the Prophets.
>
> For two whole years Paul stayed there in his own rented house and welcomed all who came to see him. Boldly and without hindrance he preached the kingdom of God and taught about the Lord Jesus Christ.

Luke 16:16

> "The Law and the Prophets were proclaimed until John. Since that time, the good news of the kingdom of God is being preached, and everyone is forcing his way into it.

As Jesus stood before Pilate for the second time, He made a revealing and dangerous admission. It was revealing because this statement provided a window into the primary purpose to His coming to Earth. It was dangerous because there were powerful, religious and political forces at work to try to find any pretext to have Him assassinated. False witnesses, lies, twisted and misrepresented statements were enlisted to inflame the Roman authorities against Him to have Him killed. The motivation for this in the natural realm was because the Jewish religious and political elite wanted to eliminate a perceived rival. In the spiritual realm the goal was to thwart God's plan to establish His Anointed One.

For years He had been a marked man. When, a few days earlier, thousands had proclaimed Him the son of David, Israel's greatest king, He became even more of a target. Up to this point Jesus had not made any statement that could have been used against him or to incriminate Him. Then, while being questioned by the Roman Governor, without any provocation and after many hours of silence, He made this profound declaration. "My Kingdom is not of this world. If it were my servants would fight to prevent my arrest by the Jews. But now my kingdom is from another place."

Pilate saw his opportunity to trap Jesus with His own words. "So you are a King?" he asked. In effect Pilate was saying, Are you saying that you are a king in Israel rather than Herod, who Rome had already endorsed and installed as its vassal?

Jesus then said what might seem strange to some Christians, but for Paul was a good confession. "It is for this reason that I came in to the world." He did not say that He came to be Savior, a suffering Servant, a substitute for our sins, although He was all of these things. Neither did He mention that He was the Lamb of God, although He was that too. In effect He told the Roman Governor that he came to assume his throne, his rule and his reign on the earth. I am a King here and now, not at some future time or in some distant place.

It was a dangerous thing to proclaim one's self a king in Caesar's realm. The emperor did not take kindly to anyone who would usurp his authority within his empire. No king would tolerate that. For Jesus to make such a statement in front of Caesar's governor was dangerous. Yet, there was a prophetic word from Pilate's wife who warned her husband to have nothing to do with this prophet because of a troubling dream that interrupted her sleep.[1] Plus, there was something about this man that gave Pilate a reason to avoid a hasty decision or judgment.

Throughout His ministry, Jesus told those He healed to keep the source of the miracles to themselves.[2] He did not want His true identity to be revealed too soon and excite opposition and resistance, especially from the religious community. He even silenced demons that blurted out who He really was[3], but, in front of Caesar's governor, He openly declared Himself God's anointed King.

I am a King here and now, not at some future time or in some distant place

Later, those who should have known and rejoiced at His arrival but were bent on His death, declared to their ultimate shame and despair, "We have no king, but Caesar."[4] They chose a substitute sovereign over the true Anointed Son of God. When Pilate realized the extent of the political pressure that these Jewish leaders were willing to bring to bear on him to crucify Jesus, he ultimately gave in and handed Him over to be executed in spite of his apprehension.

The Centerpiece of the Gospel

This statement before Pilate where Jesus admits to and proclaims His divine right to rule and reign points to the

1   Matthew 27:19
2   Two examples are Mark 1:44 and Matthew 12:15-16
3   Luke 4:32-37
4   John 19:12-16

centerpiece of His preaching, teaching and message; the foundation of the apostle Paul's gospel and a theme that moves throughout the Bible and man's history. It is called the gospel or good news that is to be to all people. It was called the Gospel of the Kingdom.

This subject is found in Genesis, both at the creation of man[5] and as the patriarch Israel addressed Judah and uttered the prophecy of the Scepter.[6] Moses was alluding to it as he prophesied about the prophet who would come after him.[7] David's throne would be the seat of His authority and he would be His son (or descendant). The Prophets proclaimed the manner,[8] circumstances of,[9] and ministry of this King.[10] A dream that disturbed King Nebuchadnezzar's sleep climaxed with God establishing His Kingdom.[11]

Before Jesus was born, angels declared Him King. He would "sit on the throne of His father David, and His Kingdom would never end." Foreign royalty, mystics and priests brought tribute, gifts and paid homage to Him at His birth. Those who saw Him as a rival, urged on by Lucifer himself, tried to end His reign by the assassination of all baby boys His age.[12]

His preaching was about the gospel of the kingdom. It is the subject of His model prayer[13] and many parables. He instructed his twelve disciples to preach that same message.[14] The seventy, who were sent out to preach later, were given the same instruction.[15] It was the new wine that had to be held in new wineskins and

---

5   Genesis 1:26-28
6   Genesis 49:10
7   Deuteronomy 18:17-19
8   Isaiah 7:14
9   Micah 5:2
10 A few are Isaiah 9:1-7, 42:1-9, 52:13-53:12, Psalm 110
11 Daniel 2
12 Matthew 1:13-18
13 Matthew 6:9-13, Luke 11:1-4
14 Matthew 9:35, Luke 9:1-2,
15 Matthew 10:1-6, Luke 10:1-12

the new fabric that could not be attached to the old.[16] Jesus said, "the law and the prophets were proclaimed until John, but since then the gospel of the Kingdom is being preached and everyone everywhere is forcing his way into it." The parable of the sower recorded in Matthew 13 describes the four responses to the message of the Kingdom. In fact, all of Matthew 13 addresses various aspects of this Kingdom in parables. This revelation, hidden from many prophets and righteous men who desperately wished to see and hear it, was revealed to the disciples and all to whom it is the Father's pleasure to unveil and give it.[17]

As Paul wrote his last letter to Timothy, he summarized the gospel he preached that had him chained like a criminal was "Jesus Christ, raised from the dead, descended from David." This made Jesus a son of David and a rightful heir to his throne. His teaching and preaching under guard from his own rented house was about the Kingdom of God and the Lord Jesus Christ.

They chose a subtitute sovereign for the true Anointed Son of God

Jesus said that "this gospel of the kingdom will be preached in the whole world as a testimony to all nations, and then the end will come." The focus of the end time prophecies of Daniel[18] and Revelation[19] also are about establishing the Kingdom of God.

This kingdom gospel was of paramount importance and central to the teaching of Jesus and the apostles. The important question is whether the gospel preached by Jesus, the apostles and Paul is being presented in its fullness today or not. If not, does it really matter? What would be the difference if it were? The purpose of this discussion is to explore these and other questions and to begin to experience the benefits of teaching and preaching

---

16 Luke 5:36-39
17 Matthew 13:16-19, 11:25-27, Luke 10:21-24, 12:32
18 Daniel 2:44-45, 7:13-14, 27
19 Revelation 5:9-10, 6:15-17, 11:15, 12:10, 19:11-16

this gospel and operating within its framework.

The first question posed is what is the Gospel of the Kingdom and upon what is it based. The following chapter will examine the conflict between it and the other competing kingdom. Then, the manifestation of the kingdom of Christ will be discussed. The following chapters will focus on the personal benefits this gospel has on the lives of believers and on their attitudes about money, wealth and prosperity. The final chapter will examine a few parables about what the revelation of this good news has on those who believe and receive it, and why many don't.

In His discussion with Nicodemus, Jesus said that unless one was born from above (or born again) they would be unable to see (or perceive) the kingdom.[20] Being a born again believer is necessary to understanding and grasping the importance of His kingdom and how it impacts a believer's everyday life. This revelation comes only by the illumination of the Holy Spirit. Without His enlightenment, it is easy to miss the implications of this awesome message.

This discussion is not about theology. It is about God's purpose and His will. Understanding the Kingdom of the Son that God loves and what it means to function in that Kingdom is essential and liberating to every believer and, for that matter, to everyone who lives on this earth. This is why it was preached everywhere to everyone. And it will be preached for a witness or testimony so that the end of the dominion of darkness can come.

The beginning of each chapter will include the passages from the Word of God that establishes its content. Take the time to carefully study each of the passages before continuing. Doing so will give the reader a head start on what will be discussed.

In many instances, the scriptures will be listed in paragraph form to show its context. This is done to guard against the misuse and misinterpretation of the Word that often can occur when isolated portions of scripture are cited out of context.

The believer's faith, which is based on the scriptures, is also essential. Faith comes by hearing and hearing by the Word of

---

20 John 3:3

God.[21] One's ears to hear the things of the Spirit are developed by spending quality time in God's Word.[22] It is the Spirit of God who speaks through the Word because it is He who inspired holy men and prophets to write; ultimately making Him its true Author. Without this spiritual sense of hearing, much of what the believer is asked to accept as fact in the Word sounds like foolishness. Spiritual things, therefore, are spiritually discerned.[23] So, to grasp the content of this work, one must be born again and receive by faith those things established from the Word of God.

Jesus began His ministry teaching the Kingdom of God. He ended His ministry with the same teaching. After His resurrection, with only a few days to prepare His witnesses and apostles to face dangers and even death before He ascended into heaven, what is the substance and content of His preparation and instruction? It is the Kingdom of God.[24]

What, then, is the Kingdom of God?

---

21 Romans 10:17
22 See The Father's Gift by S. Lloyd Walters Scepter Communications Inc. Altamonte Springs, FL 2006, 2016 for a more detailed discussion on hearing how God communicates with a believer.
23 See 1 Corinthians 1:18-2:15
24 Acts 1:3

Chapter 2

Foundation of the Kingdom

Luke 17:20-21

> Once, having been asked by the Pharisees when the kingdom of God would come, Jesus replied, "The kingdom of God does not come with your careful observation, nor will people say, 'Here it is,' or 'There it is,' because the kingdom of God is within you."

1 Samuel 16:1-2

> The Lord said to Samuel, "How long will you mourn for Saul, since I have rejected him as king over Israel? Fill your horn with oil and be on your way; I am sending you to Jesse of Bethlehem. I have chosen one of his sons to be king." But Samuel said, "How can I go? Saul will hear about it and kill me." The Lord said, "Take a heifer with you and say, 'I have come to sacrifice to the Lord.'

Daniel 4:25-26

> You will be driven away from people and will live with the wild animals; you will eat grass like cattle and be drenched with the dew of heaven. Seven times will pass by for you until you acknowledge that the Most High is sovereign over the kingdoms of men and gives them to anyone he wishes. The command to leave the stump of the tree with its roots means that your kingdom will be restored to you when you acknowledge that Heaven rules.

Psalm 33:6-9

By the word of the Lord were the heavens made, their starry host by the breath of his mouth. He gathers the waters of the sea into jars; he puts the deep into storehouses. Let all the earth fear the Lord; let all the people of the world revere him. For he spoke, and it came to be; he commanded, and it stood firm.

Hebrews 1:3

The Son is the radiance of God's glory and the exact representation of his being, sustaining all things by his powerful word. After he had provided purification for sins, he sat down at the right hand of the Majesty in heaven.

Psalm 8:3-8

When I consider your heavens, the work of your fingers, the moon and the stars, which you have set in place, what is man that you are mindful of him, the son of man that you care for him? You made him a little lower than the heavenly beings and crowned him with glory and honor. You made him ruler over the works of your hands; you put everything under his feet: all flocks and herds, and the beasts of the field, the birds of the air, and the fish of the sea, all that swim the paths of the seas.

Numbers 16:23-24, 27, 31-33

Then the Lord said to Moses, "Say to the assembly, 'Move away from the tents of Korah, Dathan and Abiram.'"

So they moved away from the tents of Korah, Dathan and Abiram. Dathan and Abiram had come out and were standing with their wives, children and little ones at the entrances to their tents.

As soon as he finished saying all this, the ground under them split apart and the earth opened its mouth and swallowed them, with their households and all Korah's men and all their possessions. They went down alive into the grave, with everything they owned; the earth closed over them, and they perished and were gone from the community.

Joshua 6:24-25

Then they burned the whole city and everything in it, but they put the silver and gold and the articles of bronze and iron into the treasury of the Lord's house. But Joshua spared Rahab the prostitute, with her family and all who belonged to her, because she hid the men Joshua had sent as spies to Jericho—and she lives among the Israelites to this day.

Romans 13:1-7

Everyone must submit himself to the governing authorities, for there is no authority except that which God has established. The authorities that exist have been established by God. Consequently, he who rebels against the authority is rebelling against what God has instituted, and those who do so will bring judgment on themselves. For rulers hold no terror for those who do right, but for those who do wrong. Do you want to be free from fear of the one in authority? Then do what is right and he will commend you. For he is God's servant to do you good. But if you do wrong, be afraid, for he does not bear the sword for nothing. He is God's servant, an agent of wrath to bring punishment on the wrongdoer. Therefore, it is necessary to submit to the authorities, not only because of possible punishment but also because of conscience. This is also why you pay taxes, for the authorities are God's servants, who give their full time to governing. Give everyone what you owe him: If you owe taxes, pay taxes; if revenue, then revenue; if respect, then respect; if honor, then honor.

Luke 7:1-10

When Jesus had finished saying all this in the hearing of the people, he entered Capernaum. There a centurion's servant, whom his master valued highly, was sick and about to die. The centurion heard of Jesus and sent some elders of the Jews to him, asking him to come and heal his servant. When they came to Jesus, they pleaded earnestly with him, "This man deserves to have you do this, because he loves our nation and has built our synagogue." So Jesus went with them. He was not far from the house when the centurion sent friends to say to him: "Lord, don't trouble yourself, for I do not deserve to have you come under my roof. That is why I did not even consider myself worthy to come to you. But say the word, and my servant will be healed. For I myself am a man under authority, with soldiers under me. I tell this one, 'Go,' and he goes; and that one, 'Come,' and he comes. I say to my servant, 'Do this,' and he does it." When Jesus heard this, he was amazed at him, and turning to the crowd following him, he said, "I tell you, I have not found such great faith even in Israel." Then the men who had been sent returned to the house and found the servant well.

Ephesians 5:22-33

Wives, submit to your husbands as to the Lord. For the husband is the head of the wife as Christ is the head of the church, his body, of which he is the Savior. Now as the church submits to Christ, so also wives should submit to their husbands in everything. Husbands, love your wives, just as Christ loved the church and gave himself up for her to make her holy, cleansing her by the washing with water through the word, and to present her to himself as a radiant church, without stain or wrinkle or any other blemish, but holy and blameless. In this same way, husbands ought to love their wives as their own bodies. He who loves his wife loves himself. After all, no one ever hated his own body, but he feeds and cares for it, just as Christ does the church—for we are members of his body. "For this reason a man will leave his father and mother and be united to his wife, and the two will become one flesh." This is a profound mystery—but I am talking about Christ and the church. However, each one of you also must love his wife as he loves himself, and the wife must respect her husband.

There are many popular definitions of the Gospel of the Kingdom. Traditionally, the church is considered His kingdom. In some Bible dictionaries and commentaries it is considered a principle or lifestyle based on the law of God.[1]

The people of Judea in the time of Christ had a more concrete concept of God's kingdom. It was the actual takeover by the Messiah politically and physically of the region of Palestine controlled by Rome.[2] This anointed King in Israel would subsequently subdue all other nations and kingdoms and exalt Jerusalem, the temple and the people connected to its worship, above all of their enemies.[3]

Jesus' disciples also took this same view. As Jesus was preparing them for his final departure after His resurrection, the disciples were still anticipating the political restoration of Israel. Even today, some view the kingdom as a political movement and entity. Many religious groups have gone to great lengths to accomplish their goals through legislation, governmental involvement, the political process and, unfortunately, military conquest.

Another popular concept is the idea of the establishment of "kingdom" people, enterprises, businesses, organizations as well as "kingdom" controlled governments. These end time views seem to be at odds with the consistent message of the prophets about a sudden, violent and cataclysmic elimination of the dominion of darkness and final territorial takeover and restoration of the Earth by the kingdom of God.[4] The kingdom of darkness will not

---

1   NIV Bible Dictionary Concordance Bible Study Helps Zondervan Grand Rapids, MI 1984

2   See Acts 1:6-8

3   This is consistent with the Hebrew end-time prophecies of Daniel, Ezekiel, Zechariah, Zephaniah, Joel and Malachi. The New Testament introduces elements alluded to in the Old Testament, such as the new covenant, the suffering and substitutionary death of the Messiah and the inclusion of gentiles in the promises given to Israel. Those prophecies are further amended and explained throughout the New Testament especially in Matthew, Romans, Hebrews, Thessalonians and Revelation.

4   Psalm 50:3-6; Daniel 2:44-45, Matthew 24:30-31, I Thessalonians 4:13-5:11

relinquish control of this world without a fight. That fight is not ours but the Lord's.

The prophets also declared that the establishment of this sovereign King will specifically be accomplished by God Himself. Believers, typified by John the Baptist and Elijah, have been proclaiming His impending arrival so that everyone who wished to might have an opportunity to prepare to meet and connect themselves to Him. Jesus specifically warned, however, that His Kingdom was not of this world, neither were its principles,[5] systems, or methods,[6] so to look for it in the world's existing structures would be a mistake.

While Jesus was in the world, He was not of the world and taught His disciples to follow His example.[7] They were to respect the authority of the state and live peaceably with all men. Their walk and lives, however, would be noticeably different. Their uniqueness would come from a Source that the world and its many influences could not duplicate.

The Kingdom Defined

What then is the Kingdom of God? Understanding this gospel hinges on understanding what is meant by the word "kingdom." There are a few instances where the term "kingdom" describes a territory ruled by a king[8] but looking at the majority of the Bible's usage of the term, especially as Jesus and the apostles describe it, the term takes on a new and more profound meaning.

Some Pharisees approached Jesus and inquired when the Kingdom of God would come. Jesus answered, "The kingdom of God does not come with your careful observation, nor will people say, 'Here it is,' or 'There it is,' because the kingdom of God is in your midst."[9]

---

5   Colossians 2:6-8, 20
6   Matthew 20:20-27
7   See John 15:18-19, 17:13-16, James4:4, 1 John 2:15-17
8   An important aspect of a king's authority is the control and protection of the borders of his realm. So the territorial dimension of the kingdom is important and significant.
9   Luke 17:20-21 (NASB), John 18:36

First, He said that the Kingdom was not in any specific location, as in a city or region. He did, however say that it was among them, meaning in their midst or vicinity. What did He mean?

A look at the concept of kingdom in 1st Samuel will help explain. As a result of Saul's disobedience and arrogance, God had become so frustrated with him that He rejected him as king. This was within two years of the prophet anointing Him king. Through the prophet Samuel, God told Saul that his kingdom over Israel would not endure and God would appoint someone after his own heart to lead his people. After Saul's further disobedience in sparing the choice livestock instead of killing everything including the Amalekites' king, Agag, as He was commanded, God commissioned Samuel to anoint David king while Saul still physically sat on the throne.[10]

The act of anointing was an outward symbol that God has chosen and empowered that specific person to rule and reign. In effect whomever God anoints has the kingdom (the dominion of a king) or the God-given right to reign and rule. The term kingdom, then, is not a place or an idea or principle or even the church. It is the vesting in a person whom God sovereignly chooses, anoints, authorizes and empowers to rule. Put another way, a kingdom is the extension of God's authority over a region, and the king is the bodily expression of that authority.

It is profoundly illustrated in the President's aircraft, Air Force One. It is considered sovereign United States' territory wherever it is. If it is in Russia, Kuwait or Israel, the plane is considered sovereign United States territory. In the movie Air Force One[11], the plane was destroyed as the President was being transferred to a military aircraft. As soon as he was personally secured on board, the designation of that aircraft was changed to Air Force One. The aircraft was just like any other military plane, but the President's presence on the plane changed the plane's designation. He has vested in his person all of the prerogatives and rights of the power

10 1 Samuel 13:1-15, 15:1-29
11 Air Force One Dir. Wolfgang Peterson. Columbia, 1997. Film.

and authority of the President of the United States of America. His mere presence changed the plane from an ordinary military transport to Air Force One.

In the story Robin Hood, King Arthur meets Robin's band of thieves in disguise. In his absence, anarchy ruled. When he revealed himself to Robin and his men, they immediately bowed and viewed his arrival as the end of the evil sheriff's reign. His presence evoked that response because the kingdom, the power to rule and reign, is vested in the person of the king.

Saul understood this. He would later tell his son, Jonathan, to bring his beloved friend, David to him so that he could kill him, for as long as David lived, he said, Jonathan could not establish his kingdom or right to rule.[12] Saul was on the throne, but God had placed the authority and prerogative to reign on David. Saul's solution to that problem was to eliminate David by assassination. The kingdom can only be destroyed by the death of the king.

A kingdom is the extension of God's authority over a region and the king is the bodily expression of that authority

Favor followed David. God worked mightily in his behalf. The people loved him. Even members of Saul's family loved him. God anointed him. He had the right to reign. He did not yet sit on the throne or enjoy the wealth and comforts of the palace, but he had the kingdom, or the God-given prerogative to rule and reign as king, conferred upon him.

Another example of this is found in the book of Daniel.[13] Because of his pride, Nebuchadnezzar's kingdom was taken from him for seven years. For that period he lost his sanity, ate grass like a beast of the field, and was driven from among the people.

12 1 Samuel 20:31
13 Daniel 4

After that time was concluded, his kingdom, or right and ability to rule and reign, was restored when his sanity returned. The kingdom was attached to his person (sanity, glory, honor, majesty, etc.) and was given him by God, who could also take it back. He sets up kings and deposes them,[14] and Nebuchadnezzar learned that lesson firsthand.

That is what Jesus meant when He told the Pharisees that the Kingdom was in their midst. The King was standing there talking to them, so the One with the right to rule and reign was in their midst. He had come to pick up the scepter of rulership that Adam lost.

Adam, the First King

At creation, God appointed Adam to have dominion and rule over all of the works of his hands. Everything was to be under Adam's feet. This planet and everything in it was his domain, and he was its king. God vested in him the authority over the territory and realm that He had created. That authority carried with it certain awesome responsibilities. His decisions affected everything and everyone within his domain. This is the way God does things. He placed the man He created as the head over all things in the earth.

God is the Head of all things in the universe and He wanted to create a being like Himself. He was a Being that could make choices, reproduce and speak with authority; a being after His likeness and His image. A being, who, like His Father, would work and rest and give names to things under his dominion. A being that would rule and reign.

God is a spirit. The angels are as well. This new being, however, would be different. He would be a spirit being housed in a body made of flesh. By His own command, God had established that the one who would have dominion and rulership of this realm

---

14   Daniel 2:19-23 (See also Jeremiah 27:4-11)

would be man; again, a spirit being housed in flesh.[15] This is an important distinction. Angels and even He Himself, who both operate in the invisible realm, could only have access to this visible realm with the consent of man. Adam, then, would bridge the gulf between the visible and the invisible realms. After the creation of man, God would only act in the earth through man and only by his permission. This explains one of the reasons why it was an absolute imperative for Jesus to be a flesh and blood man.

The Power of Words

This regal authority would be exercised through the things that Adam said. All of the words the man would speak and the actions He would take would affect everyone and everything under his authority. The power and impact of words spoken cannot be underestimated. At creation God spoke and inanimate matter and substance obeyed His commands. When He spoke the word "light," illumination emerged and separated itself from darkness. God's authority is resident in His Word. He upholds all things by the word of His power. He doesn't just speak His word. He sends His Word and then watches over it to see that it performs the purposes for which it was sent.[16]

The son of God formed of the dust of the ground on the sixth day of creation was to walk in that same authority. Everything on the Earth was under his authority — and everything meant everything: animals, winds and waves, all of creation.

The Son who came through Mary walked in that same authority. In fact, many of the miracles that He performed were exercises of authority rather than demonstrations of power. When He spoke to a storm to quiet its commotion, the winds and the waves yielded to His command.[17] When He told sickness

---

15 A great debt is owed to Dr. Myles Munroe for this teaching. For further study see his book The Power and Purpose of Prayer Destiny Image, New Kensington, PA 2000
16 Isaiah 55:8-11
17 Matthew 8:23-27

and disease to depart, viruses to leave, growths to go away, bones to straighten and correct themselves, cancerous and mutated cells to dissolve, each would immediately comply. A fig tree which He cursed dried up from its roots in obedience.[18] Demons[19] and even the dead responded to his voice.[20]

When He taught, His words carried a certain gravitas. His own disciples marveled at the capacity He had to command inanimate nature, fish, disease, demons and even death would obey Him. He was a man, but not like any other man that they had ever encountered. They were seeing a man who understood His authority and properly exercised it.

He said that all He was doing was what he saw the Father do.[21] This was what the first Adam, the last Adam and all of the sons that followed Him was to be able to do as well.

Suzerain and Vassal

The establishment of the kings of Israel and Judah, although done over God's objections, modeled the covenant relationships of a suzerain and a vassal. A great king, known as a suzerain, who possessed great wealth and military might, would initiate an agreement or covenant between himself and a lesser king, known as a vassal. The vassal's responsibility was to remain completely loyal and obedient to this covenant relationship. In return the suzerain would protect and provide for the needs of the vassal. Any violation of these conditions would abrogate and cancel the covenant relationship and, in some instances, have dire consequences. They would refer to each other as lord and servant and, as the relationship grew, as father and son.[22]

Any attack on the vassal's person, authority, rule or realm was an attack or insult to the suzerain, who would be obligated

18   Matthew 21:18-22, Mark 11:12-14, 20-25
19   Matthew 8:28-34, 9:32-33, Mark 1:23-26, 9:17-29
20   Matthew 9:18-19, 23-25, Luke 7:11-15, John 11:1-44
21   John 5:19-23
22   NIV Study Bible Zondervan Grand Rapids, MI 1973, 1995, 2005 page 18

to respond to the offending person or nation with the full extent of his power. The suzerain-vassal covenant relationship was the model of both the kingdoms of Israel and Judah as well as God and Adam. It was also the basis for the concept of the divine right of kings throughout the middle ages and into modern times. This is where the idea of the "divine right of kings" originated and is still in existence today.

Kingdom, the power to rule and reign is vested in the person of the king

God's revelation about Nebuchadnezzar through the prophet Jeremiah provides a vivid example of this suzerain and vassal relationship between a deity and a king.

> Early in the reign of Zedekiah son of Josiah king of Judah, this word came to Jeremiah from the Lord: This is what the Lord said to me: "Make a yoke out of straps and crossbars and put it on your neck. Then send word to the kings of Edom, Moab, Ammon, Tyre and Sidon through the envoys who have come to Jerusalem to Zedekiah king of Judah. Give them a message for their masters and say, 'This is what the Lord Almighty, the God of Israel, says: "Tell this to your masters: With my great power and outstretched arm I made the earth and its people and the animals that are on it, and I give it to anyone I please. Now I will hand all your countries over to my servant Nebuchadnezzar king of Babylon; I will make even the wild animals subject to him.[23]

The prophet announced to the representatives of five kings and king Zedekiah, king of Judah, that God would hand all of their masters' kingdoms over to the control and authority of Nebuchadnezzar, king of Babylon. The language of the announcement was audacious. Jehovah declared that He could

---

23 Jeremiah 27:4-11

do this because He made the earth and its people and animals that are on it by His mighty hand and power. It's My prerogative. The ultimate Suzerain (God) had announced and established His vassal (Nebuchadnezzar), who became suzerain over all the other nations.

Nebuchadnezzar's authority, according to God, extended even to the wild animals. This shows how broad and extensive the authority of a king under God's authority reaches. We saw the full expression of this when Jesus appeared on the earth.

Also, notice that God calls Nebuchadnezzar "My servant." God reserves this title to those who hold high positions or walk in great authority in His kingdom. He generally referred to prophets and kings as His servants. In the New Testament apostles call themselves servants of God or the Lord Jesus Christ. This is not a title taken lightly. Often before that designation is ascribed to someone, they will have been thoroughly tested and tried by God, and only after they have proven themselves and have been extensively vetted, wiil they be referred to as servants.

Nebuchadnezzar's situation, however, is quite different. At the time of this announcement, he was a heathen king who did not even know God. This certainly would have created some doubt in the minds of the Israelites about the credibility and veracity of Jeremiah's prophetic office and word. How could a brutal and heathen foreign king, who did not believe in nor worship Jehovah and was attacking the children of Israel, be a servant of God?

God has always engaged kings of all types either on behalf of his people or to introduce Himself to that king. He sent dreams to Abimelech regarding Abram[24] and to Pharaoh for Joseph to interpret.[25] He did the same thing to Nebuchadnezzar with Daniel. He sent prophets to Israelite kings[26] as well as to heathen neighboring kings throughout Israel and Judah's history.[27] God

---

24 Genesis 20
25 Genesis 41
26 See the Prophecies of Dan, Nathan, Elijah, Elisha and others in 1 and 2 Samuel, Kings Chronicles, etc.
27 See the prophecies of Isaiah, Daniel, Jeremiah, Jonah, and Nahum.

honors protocol by communicating His purposes and will to
the sovereigns of the nations through His prophets, apostles
or directly through dreams and visions. Ultimately, they are all
answerable to Him.

Often, kings would have disputes that would lead to warfare.
In effect these conflicts between kings were actually contests
between deities. One king would claim that his deity had given
him certain territories while the other king would assert that his
deity had given them to him. War would test the legitimacy of a
king's rule, kingdom and territory. As stated earlier, the suzerain
is responsible to enforce his vassal's right to rule and reign. The
king that won would prove the supremacy of his claim and his
deity by the defeat and death of the opposing king.

these conflict between kings were actually contests between dieties

When the Philistines fought against Israel, this scenario
is once again played out.[28] The champion of the Philistines
challenged the Israelites to battle one-on-one. This was not just
a test of physical prowess or expertise in hand-to-hand combat,
it was a contest between deities. It was about whose god was
superior to the other, and whose god could grant his vassal the
victory. While Saul, who was the king, was hesitant to stand up to
the Philistine's imposing warrior, David took the giant's insults as
an affront to his God, Jehovah. Note that David had already been
anointed, and the prerogatives and protections due a king already
rested on him. God was obliged to stand with His vassal. When
Goliath saw this young man without any armor or conventional
implements of war, he made light of his youthful opponent and
suggested he would make quick work of David. David made clear
that his confidence was in his God and not in swords and shields.
He even threw out some insults of his own before attacking his
opponent in a full sprint. David's stunning victory over Goliath

---

28 1 Samuel 17

convinced the horrified Philistines of the supremacy of the Israelites' God, revealed and introduced this little shepherd boy to the masses in Israel, and excited the jealousy and animosity of king Saul who now realized that this young man was not merely Jesse's son or the army's newest warrior. He was a rival to the throne. And he was right.

Headship

Headship is a reoccurring theme in the Bible. It appears in many forms. It is seen in God's dealings with the many kings of Israel and Judah, in the family structure and in the church. It was even highlighted when the congregation rebelled against His appointed leader, Moses, in the wilderness.

The headship principle exists even within the Godhead. Although the Father, the Son and the Holy Ghost are equal in every way, the Father assumes the role as Head. The Son, who submits to the Father, takes an authoritative role with the Holy Ghost.

This is the model for the first family. Adam was the head and the one responsible and answerable to God. This did not make Eve inferior to Him. She was part of him and equal to him, yet God sovereignly placed the responsibility for decision-making, with all of the accountability that came with it, upon the man. They both then exercise authority over the children and any outside influences

In the church, God appoints Apostles, Prophets, Evangelists and Pastor / Teachers. These ascension gifts are given to the church for spiritual headship authority over people. Please note the distinction between these offices and the Bishops and Deacons.[29] God sovereignly selects and appoints the ascension gifts. The people of the church vote on and select Bishops and Deacons.

29 1 Timothy 3:1-10

He came to retreive the scepter of rulership that Adam lost

In the home, God looks to the man to lead, and He holds him responsible for that flock. The husband and wife share the parenting responsibilities and authority over the children who must obey their parents.[30]

In the wilderness, when Korah, Dathan and Abiram rebelled against Moses and Aaron, God's attitude toward His established order of headship is vividly illustrated. God arbitrarily chose those who would lead the entire congregation of Israel. He asked no one's opinion and took no vote. There was no committee involved in their selection. He looks into places that man's eyes cannot see when He chooses his leaders. He looks at the heart.[31] God selected who he decided would lead the multitude in the wilderness — Moses, Aaron and Miriam,[32] with Moses as head.

These members of the tribe of Levi, who were of the same tribe as Moses and Aaron, saw things differently. They felt that they were just as capable of leadership as these two brothers and stood against them. God then stepped into the dispute.

The structural order of authority was challenged. God took that personally, and He answered the rebellion in the same way that He dealt with any other violation of His headship order. He commanded that the leaders of the usurpation of Moses' and Aaron's authority stand at the doors of their respective tents with all that belonged to them. Their wives children, dogs, cats, followers, etc. were all with them. They were the heads, and what they did and said affected everything that was connected to them.

Suddenly, the ground opened up and swallowed tents, people, furniture, dogs and cats together into the ground. It closed upon them burying everyone alive. Even in punishment, God honored His principle of headship. This highlights the importance and

---

30 Ephesians 6:1, Colossians 3:20
31 1 Samuel 16:1-7
32 Micah 6:4

responsibility of being the head. Whether one is the head of a home, congregation city or a nation, that person carries the responsibility of all who are under their authority on their shoulders. It is a privilege, but a heavy responsibility.

This is both positive and negative. With Rahab, the woman that housed and protected the Israelite spies as they scouted Jericho, her entire household benefitted from her actions. Everyone who "belonged" to her was spared the fate of the rest of those who lived in Jericho because of her kindness.[33] Who one "belongs" to then, is important as will be seen in future chapters.

The severity of the sentence carried out on the rebellion in the wilderness shows Gods' attitude toward any violation of the principle of headship that He has established. Lucifer violated it in heaven. Many violate it in the church, the home, and even in society. If a child rebelled against parental authority in Israel while in the wilderness, that child was taken outside the camp and stoned to death.[34]

All authority comes from God, even civil authority. The teacher, the police officer, the principal, the judge, the mayor, the governor, the president, all receive their authority from God. Standing before Pilate, Jesus pointed out that Pilate could only do what His Father permitted him to do. As a man subject to human authority, Jesus, in obedience to the Father, subjected Himself to Pilate's order to be crucified.

Submission

In God's order of things one is to submit to those who he has placed in authority. The Son submits to the Father. The Holy Ghost submits to the Son. The church submits to the Holy Ghost. The members of the body (the church) submit to the Deacon. The Deacon submits to the Elder. The Elder submits to the Bishop. The Bishop submits to the Prophet and the Apostle. The wife

---

33 The fact that Rahab, who was both a woman and a gentile, showed that faith in God transcended all aspects of the flesh including gender, national, racial and ethnic origin is also found in the Old Testament.

34 See Deuteronomy 21:18-23

submits to the husband. The children submit to their mother and father. God created this order and expects it to be faithfully followed. Any deviation from this creates disorder and God will always put things back in order one way or another.

There is a profound difference between submission and obedience. Even though one obeys, even though they are compliant, they may not be submissive. A spirit of defiance or disrespect may accompany one's acquiescence. Submission, however, acknowledges authority and humbly yields. The attitude to the one in authority is key.

This does not excuse the leader from manipulative and abusive leadership. Many in the home, church, business, politics, education, etc. use their position of leadership to physically and psychologically abuse those under their charge. God may give the leader warnings and time to correct the error of their way. Eventually, if the leader refuses or is unable to make the necessary changes, one of two things will happen; either the leader will be replaced one way or another as was the case with Saul, or the people will leave the leader to rule over an empty realm as was the case with the Pharaoh in Egypt after the children of Israel left.

The Kingdom of God, then, is vested in the one that God anointed as his appointed Head or King of all things. Everything has been placed under His feet. He is far above all rule, authority, power and dominion.[35] His name is above every name.[36] He has been given authority over life and death, and to judge the living and the dead.[37] All of this has been done at the pleasure of the Father.

There was, however, opposition. It began before time, and the problems we now face in the earth can be traced to rebellion against God's ordained order.

---

35 Ephesians 1:17-23
36 Philippians 2:6-11
37 See John 5:16-30

Chapter 3

Kingdoms in Conflict

Revelation 12:7-12

> And there was war in heaven. Michael and his angels fought against the dragon, and the dragon and his angels fought back. But he was not strong enough, and they lost their place in heaven. The great dragon was hurled down—that ancient serpent called the devil, or Satan, who leads the whole world astray. He was hurled to the earth, and his angels with him. Then I heard a loud voice in heaven say: "Now have come the salvation and the power and the kingdom of our God, and the authority of his Christ. For the accuser of our brothers, who accuses them before our God day and night, has been hurled down. They overcame him by the blood of the Lamb and by the word of their testimony; they did not love their lives so much as to shrink from death. Therefore rejoice, you heavens and you who dwell in them! But woe to the earth and the sea, because the devil has gone down to you! He is filled with fury, because he knows that his time is short."

1 Samuel 15:23

> For rebellion is like the sin of divination, and arrogance like the evil of idolatry. Because you have rejected the word of the Lord, he has rejected you as king."

Matthew 4:1-11

> Then Jesus was led by the Spirit into the desert to be tempted

by the devil. After fasting forty days and forty nights, he was hungry. The tempter came to him and said, "If you are the Son of God, tell these stones to become bread." Jesus answered, "It is written: 'Man does not live on bread alone, but on every word that comes from the mouth of God.'" Then the devil took him to the holy city and had him stand on the highest point of the temple. "If you are the Son of God," he said, "throw yourself down. For it is written: "'He will command his angels concerning you, and they will lift you up in their hands, so that you will not strike your foot against a stone.'" Jesus answered him, "It is also written: 'Do not put the Lord your God to the test.'" Again, the devil took him to a very high mountain and showed him all the kingdoms of the world and their splendor. "All this I will give you," he said, "if you will bow down and worship me." Jesus said to him, "Away from me, Satan! For it is written: 'Worship the Lord your God, and serve him only.'" Then the devil left him, and angels came and attended him.

Luke 4:1-13

Jesus, full of the Holy Spirit, returned from the Jordan and was led by the Spirit in the desert, where for forty days he was tempted by the devil. He ate nothing during those days, and at the end of them he was hungry. The devil said to him, "If you are the Son of God, tell this stone to become bread." Jesus answered, "It is written: 'Man does not live on bread alone.'" The devil led him up to a high place and showed him in an instant all the kingdoms of the world. And he said to him, "I will give you all their authority and splendor, for it has been given to me, and I can give it to anyone I want to. So if you worship me, it will all be yours." Jesus answered, "It is written: 'Worship the Lord your God and serve him only.'" The devil led him to Jerusalem and had him stand on the highest point of the temple. "If you are the Son of God," he said, "throw yourself down from here. For it is written: "'He will command his angels concerning you to guard you carefully; they will lift you up in their hands, so that you will not strike your foot against a stone.'" Jesus answered, "It says: 'Do not put the Lord your God to the test.'" When the devil had finished all this tempting, he left him until an opportune time.

Ezekiel 28:11-19

The word of the Lord came to me: "Son of man, take up a lament concerning the king of Tyre and say to him: 'This is what the Sovereign Lord says: "'You were the model of perfection, full of wisdom and perfect in beauty. You were in Eden, the garden of God; every precious stone adorned you: ruby, topaz and emerald, chrysolite, onyx and jasper, sapphire, turquoise and beryl. Your settings and mountings were made of gold; on the day you were created they were prepared. You were anointed as a guardian cherub, for so I ordained you. You were on the holy mount of God; you walked among the fiery stones. You were blameless in your ways from the day you were created till wickedness was found in you. Through your widespread trade you were filled with violence, and you sinned. So I drove you in disgrace from the mount of God, and I expelled you, O guardian cherub, from among the fiery stones. Your heart became proud on account of your beauty, and you corrupted your wisdom because of your splendor. So I threw you to the earth; I made a spectacle of you before kings. By your many sins and dishonest trade you have desecrated your sanctuaries. So I made a fire come out from you, and it consumed you, and I reduced you to ashes on the ground in the sight of all who were watching. All the nations who knew you are appalled at you; you have come to a horrible end and will be no more.'"

Isaiah 14:12-14

How you have fallen from heaven, O morning star, son of the dawn! You have been cast down to the earth, you who once laid low the nations! You said in your heart, "I will ascend to heaven; I will raise my throne above the stars of God; I will sit enthroned on the mount of assembly, on the utmost heights of the sacred mountain. I will ascend above the tops of the clouds; I will make myself like the Most High."

Genesis 3:1-19

Now the serpent was more crafty than any of the wild animals the Lord God had made. He said to the woman, "Did God really say, 'You must not eat from any tree in the garden'?" The woman said to the serpent, "We may eat fruit from the trees in the garden, but God did say, 'You must not eat fruit from the tree that is in the middle of the garden, and you must not touch it, or you will die.'" "You will not surely die," the serpent said to the woman. "For God knows that when you eat of it your eyes will be opened, and you will be like God, knowing good and evil." When the woman saw that the fruit of the tree was good for food and pleasing to the eye, and also desirable for gaining wisdom, she took some and ate it. She also gave some to her husband, who was with her, and he ate it. Then the eyes of both of them were opened, and they realized they were naked; so they sewed fig leaves together and made coverings for themselves. Then the man and his wife heard the sound of the Lord God as he was walking in the garden in the cool of the day, and they hid from the Lord God among the trees of the garden. But the Lord God called to the man, "Where are you?" He answered, "I heard you in the garden, and I was afraid because I was naked; so I hid." And he said, "Who told you that you were naked? Have you eaten from the tree that I commanded you not to eat from?" The man said, "The woman you put here with me—she gave me some fruit from the tree, and I ate it." 13 Then the Lord God said to the woman, "What is this you have done?" The woman said, "The serpent deceived me, and I ate." So the Lord God said to the serpent, "Because you have done this, "Cursed are you above all the livestock and all the wild animals! You will crawl on your belly and you will eat dust all the days of your life. And I will put enmity between you and the woman, and between your offspring and hers; he will crush your head, and you will strike his heel." To the woman he said, "I will greatly increase your pains in childbearing; with pain you will give birth to children. Your desire will be for your husband, and he will rule over you." To Adam he said, "Because you listened to your wife and ate from the tree about which I commanded you, 'You must not eat of it,' "Cursed is the ground because of you; through painful toil you will eat of it all the days of your life. It will produce thorns and thistles for you, and you will eat the plants of the field. By the sweat of your brow you will eat your food until you return to the ground, since from it you were taken; for dust you are and to dust you will return."

Matthew 8:28-29, 10:1-8

> When he arrived at the other side in the region of the Gadarenes, two demon-possessed men coming from the tombs met him. They were so violent that no one could pass that way. "What do you want with us, Son of God?" they shouted. "Have you come here to torture us before the appointed time?"
>
> He called his twelve disciples to him and gave them authority to drive out evil spirits and to heal every disease and sickness. These are the names of the twelve apostles: first, Simon (who is called Peter) and his brother Andrew; James son of Zebedee, and his brother John; Philip and Bartholomew; Thomas and Matthew the tax collector; James son of Alphaeus, and Thaddaeus; Simon the Zealot and Judas Iscariot, who betrayed him. These twelve Jesus sent out with the following instructions: "Do not go among the Gentiles or enter any town of the Samaritans. Go rather to the lost sheep of Israel. As you go, preach this message: 'The kingdom of heaven is near.' Heal the sick, raise the dead, cleanse those who have leprosy, drive out demons. Freely you have received, freely give.

Luke 11:20

> But if I drive out demons by the finger of God, then the kingdom of God has come to you.

The Bible states it simply: "There was war in heaven." The image that is conjured up when one thinks of heaven is, in a word, paradise. It is a place with streets made out of gold instead of asphalt. Gates are made out of a single pearl and walls consisting of jasper instead of cinder blocks, wood and sheet rock. The foundations of the city are not made of concrete poured out of a cement truck, but various precious stones. There is no imperfection there. There are trees, flowers, and plants that never fade or die. Some trees bear a different fruit each month. It is viewed as an utterly positive and perfectly ordered environment; paradise.

But, the Bible says, there was war in heaven. The environment created, structured and maintained by God was disrupted. His authority was usurped. His order was challenged. His character was questioned. Out of this conflict two kingdoms emerged, each opposed to the other, whose characteristics are direct opposites of each other. Eventually, all of the inhabitants of the earth, where the battle is now being waged, will choose one kingdom and its king, or the other.

The leader of this rebellion is well known. His name was Lucifer, son of the morning. He was created as a intelligent, beautiful, talented and with the highest honor among those who ministered to the Most High God. His pipes, or vocal organs gave him exceptional musical abilities. His beauty surpassed anything that had been created, and he was a covering cherub. He was privileged to minister in the presence of the Almighty with duties similar to those of an honor guard that attends a great head of state or monarch.

One of the other archangels is known as Michael. The name Michael means one like God. This archangel Michael appears many times in the Word of God. He disputes with the accuser, Satan, over the body of Moses.[1] He comes to Gabriel's aid with the Persians and then is referred to as a Prince when he stands up for the people of God.[2] It is Michael who commands the angels

---

1   Jude 9
2   Daniel 10:12-11:1, 12:1-4

who fight against Lucifer's rebellion in heaven.[3]

The patriarchs Abraham[4] and Jacob encountered God and angels who appeared as men. Jacob wrestled with an Angel, yet says and is supported in Hosea[5] that he wrestled with and saw the face of God and lived, as did Gideon and Samson's parents, Manoah and his wife.[6] Often in the Old Testament this angel, called the Angel of the Lord, speaks with God's authority.

As Joshua was doing reconnaissance of Jericho, he encountered a man with his sword drawn. "Are you for us or for our enemies?" Joshua asked. "Neither" replied the man, "But as commander of the army of the Lord, I have now come." This man then commanded Joshua, using the same language that was used when Moses approached the burning bush,[7] to remove his sandals because the ground that he was standing on was holy ground. Joshua complied and bowed to worship this commander of the armies of the Lord.[8]

God will restore His order one way or another

God the Father has always chosen to act through His Son. Throughout John, the Spirit revealed that the Father acted through Jesus in creation and in the earth. Is it possible that He acted through Jesus to represent Himself to the angels like He represents Him to us? Is it possible that this Michael, this one like God, this commander of the armies of the Lord who expelled Lucifer from heaven, is really the second person of the

---

3   Revelation 12:7-9
4   Genesis 18:1-33, 32:1
5   Hosea 12:4
6   Genesis 32:22-30, Judges 6:11-24, 13:1-24
7   Exodus 3:4-5
8   Joshua 5:13-15

Godhead?[9] No angel would have accepted worship from Joshua. When John did it, he was quickly corrected.[10] This same Michael commanded the host of angels who hurled Lucifer like lightening out of heaven.

The man with the curly white hair and bronze legs that John and Daniel saw accepted worship. Could that also be Michael? Interestingly, the being who appeared to Daniel on the banks of the river Tigris before the angel comes to interpret the vision remarkably resembles the son of man John saw on Patmos. If this was Michael, the access and privileges to the Father made available to this archangel and, rightfully, withheld from Lucifer could explain, yet not justify, his jealousy. And it would be something if the same commander of the Lord's hosts that handled him so convincingly in Heaven is personally handling him here on earth as well?[11]

The Roots of the Rebellion

The roots of the conflict originate within Lucifer's inner desire for self-promotion and exultation. Being the highest-ranking angel was not enough. He decided that he deserved a promotion. By his own estimation, he was experienced, qualified and intelligent enough to sit where God sat. Plus, there were things that probably should be done differently, if not better, from Lucifer's point of view. Some things did not make sense to him nor meet with his enlightened approval.

Lucifer's pride, self-importance and arrogance led him into open rebellion against God. He became dissatisfied with his God-given role, and in doing so, he violated God's order and challenged

9   Notice that the Angel of the Lord spoke in the first person to Hagar about the promises made to Abraham (Genesis 16:7-12).
10   Revelation 22:8-9
11   This discussion about Michael the archangel, while not absolutely central the idea of the gospel of the kingdom, does provide an interesting insight into the subject. It does not, however, suggest any hint of Arianism. Assuming the role of an angel does not make the second Person of the Godhead any less God than assuming the role of a man. It only serves to further highlight His humility and willingness to serve.

His authority. As already illustrated, God will restore His order one way or another. The Father's solution was unambiguous and severe. Lucifer and all who followed him were forcibly ejected and expelled from heaven.

Lucifer's rebellion in heaven created, in essence, a second kingdom or dominion that God has allowed to develop. This kingdom is based on and has the characteristics of its head. It is in nature and goals completely opposed to God's kingdom. The darkness of Lucifer's dominion only makes the brightness of the kingdom of God shine in greater brilliance.

The basic difference between the dominion of darkness and kingdom of light is that Lucifer's kingdom is directed inward to self while God's kingdom is directed outward to others. The spirit of the dominion of darkness is always about my need, my wants, my tastes, my desires, etc. It's me first, my supremacy, my glory.

This spirit of Lucifer is seen everywhere in his dominion and can even infect religion. Some religions depict God as self-absorbed, mean, and only interested in being appeased, making God appear self-serving. This pattern is repeated over and over again in many pagan religions, and this is the same lie that was told in heaven and to Eve through a serpent in the Garden of Eden. As he tried to lure Eve into eating the forbidden fruit, Lucifer accused God of denying her something beneficial and keeping it for Himself.

The spirit of self is also seen in many who depict the goal of salvation as getting things: houses, cars, money, etc. God does bless materially, however, that is not His goal. The spirit of greed and the love of money come from the same source – Lucifer.

Another internal desire that feeds the spirit of self is pride. There are all types of pride everywhere. The severest form of pride, arrogance, is on display in every corner of society. From Wall Street to Martin Luther King Boulevard, this spirit can be clearly seen.

It is even in the church world in the form of church pride This pride can be produced by doctrinal beliefs, pride in the size of one's church, pride in the charisma of the pastor, or even pride in the manifestation of supernatural signs, wonders and miracles one might be able to perform individually or in the context of a particular ministry. When the effect of the spirit produced in that ministry is "I or we are better than you" or more holy or more authentic, that spirit may be a prideful spirit.

The kingdom of God, by contrast, is characterized by self-sacrifice, vividly personified in Jesus. In Philippians 2, the Holy Spirit through Paul showed the true character of Jesus and His kingdom.[12] Although He was equal with God, Jesus made of Himself no reputation and took the stance of a servant. He humbled Himself even to a horrible death on a cross. God then exalted Him. Lucifer exalted himself, but Jesus humbled Himself, and as a result, He was exalted.

Lucifer's rebellion in heaven created second kingdom

As Jesus and His disciples assembled for what has become known as the "Last Supper", He got water and a towel. He removed His outer clothing and knelt at each of the disciples' feet. Because the common footwear of the time was an open sandal, one's feet would become soiled with the dust of the dirt roads as well as anything else that would drop or drip from the donkeys and horses that used those same roads. As he made His way around the table washing the grit and grime off of each disciple's feet, the water and towel would show the effects of the collective filth. When it was Peter's turn, he looked at the mocha colored water, the spotted towel, then, to his Lord and objected.

Peter, who, under the influence of the Spirit of God, declared Jesus to be the Christ, the Son of the Living God, saw Jesus' washing of His subordinate's feet as demeaning, humiliating and beneath the dignity of a king — his king. That, however, was one of the points that Jesus was making. The Word teaches that one

---

12 Philippians 2:5-11

should not think more of himself than he ought.[13] Yet, if anyone could make much of himself, it would have been Jesus. He was the model of humility.[14] He taught, by his actions, that in His Kingdom, whoever is the greatest is the servant[15] and the youngest.[16]

The one word characteristic of the Kingdom of God is love – a love that is not self-seeking,[17] but seeks the good of others.[18] Is not puffed up or boastful.[19] It is out of the Father's love that His Son was freely given as payment for the sins of the whole world. He gave His only Son, whom He loved, so that others might have life.[20] No greater love has ever been expressed than a man would give up his life for a friend, not to mention those who may yet be enemies.[21] The focus of and the spirit of the kingdom of light is to serve others in love.

Self Determination

The rebellion that began in heaven spread to the earth by Adam's decision to submit to Lucifer. The spirit of this kingdom once again is focused on self or, more specifically, self-determination. The temptation in the Garden of Eden centered on whether to let God determine what they would do or whether they would make that determination for themselves.

The fruit of one tree in the middle of the garden was forbidden as a source for food by God's command. Adam was specifically warned that eating of the fruit of that tree would bring death. The lure of satisfying one's taste, and senses, as well as the desire to gain wisdom and knowledge that would take him to a new level all appealed to self. Apparently, he did not consider whether this

---

13 Romans 12:3, Galatians 6:3-5
14 Philippians 2:5-11
15 Matthew 20:26-28
16 Luke 22:24-27
17 1 Corinthians 13:4-7
18 1 Corinthians 10:24
19 1 Corinthians 13:4-7
20 John 3:16-17
21 John 15:9-13, Matthew 5:43-48

new level was beneficial or not. Adam, who stood silently as Eve ate of the fruit, understood the consequences of the act. When he took the fruit, he made a conscious choice to satisfy his palate, enrich himself with new knowledge, and, ultimately, determined that he would be his own authority.

The question, "Who told you that you were naked?" reveals that God intended for man's only authoritative source was to be His voice. He never intended for man to weigh whether a thing was good or bad. Adam's mentioning that he was naked revealed that he was not only self-conscious of his attire, but had determined that it was inappropriate for him to approach God that way. He was receiving his information from another source, and he acted on it. For many afternoons from the day of his creation, he greeted God comfortably without any covering over his naked body, now he felt shame and embarrassment. He had entered territory for which he was unprepared.

God reserved the knowledge of good and evil and its consequences to Himself. That was for man's protection. All that man had to do was follow God's leading and all of the privileges; blessings and honor bestowed upon them would remain unchanged. Adams' choice was between determining for himself what to do with the tree or walking in God's choices for him.

Lucifer's kingdom is directed inward toward self, God's Kingdom is directed outward toward others

It was, therefore, never God's intent for man to know good or evil, only His voice. Note that when one sees his own goodness, one tends to notice someone else's evil and become judgmental. So, even the knowledge of good was not revealed. The walk of the new covenant believer that is led by the Spirit will get closer to this original intent of the Father. What He always wanted the believer to know exclusively was His voice and life, not good, evil or death.

By choosing to submit to the voice of the serpent through his wife, Adam yielded himself, Eve and all that was under his authority and dominion to Lucifer. With a foothold in the earth, the effects of the dominion of darkness were introduced. Disease, decay and death were manifested. The rebellion had now spread to the earth, and the principles of Lucifer's kingdom were on display in the earth and its inhabitants.

Before expelling Adam and Eve from the garden, God revealed a contingency plan devised before creation that would recapture what had been lost. One of Adam's descendants would be struck in the heel by the serpent, but he would crush the serpent's head. Anticipating His arrival, men began to "call on the name of the Lord."[22] The two kingdoms, God's and Lucifer's now would wage war on earth: The same war that began in heaven was now being waged in this new realm.

The Kingdom of God is characterized by self-sacrifice

The stakes are high in this war. Every aspect of life on the earth is involved. It is not just religious, but social, geopolitical, scientific, educational, ecological and psychological, in its implications. Behind every minor skirmish in the school yard or international conflict is this conflict between the anointed King of God's Kingdom, Christ Jesus and Lucifer. No one is neutral or a bystander.

Everyone who is born on this planet begins in opposition to God's Kingdom due to Adam's choice. If no choice is made, one will remain under the dominion of darkness and receive the fate awaiting Lucifer. However, if one enters into the Kingdom of God's beloved Son, they will enjoy His fate. Remember, one will

22 Genesis 4:26

receive the fate of the head to which they are connected.

When Jesus encountered two demon-possessed men in the Gadarenes, the demons within them, acknowledging His authority, cried out, "What do you want with us, Son of God. Have you come to torture us before the appointed time?" The forces of Lucifer were expecting the anointed King of God's Kingdom. Every possible method had been employed to prevent His arrival. Murdering baby boys, attempting to wipe out whole families, seduction by power, lust, fortune, and by any means at his disposal, Lucifer tried to forestall or even abort the birth of Christ Jesus, to no avail.

The Old Testament record was the basis of the many factions of Judaism in Jesus' day, and each felt that their particular brand of religion was authentic and sanctioned by God. Jesus pointed out, however, that the record of the Scriptures was about Him, His arrival and kingdom. He said,

> You diligently study the Scriptures because you think
> that by them you possess eternal life. These are the
> Scriptures that testify about me, yet you refuse to come
>
> to me to have life.[23]

You think that you have found life in the many doctrines and dogma of your teachings, but the record you read is really all pointing to me. It is all about me, and life. The life that you seek is only found in me. Yet, you will not come to me to have that life.

The encounter between Christ and Satan was a negotiation between the combatants

There is a similar, if not a worse, situation today. With multiple brands of "Christian" churches, ministries and denominations, each emphasizing a particular and peculiar, unique point, position

---

23 John 5:39-40

or practice, the real Subject of the word is lost. It is and always has been about the Christ and nothing else. In the presence of Israel's great lawgiver, Moses and their greatest prophet, Elijah, the Father said "He is my Beloved Son; listen to Him."[24]

The Three Temptations of Christ

Once He arrived and after He was baptized, Jesus went face to face with His enemy in the wilderness. The three temptations that He faced went to the very heart of the conflict. They were, in fact, more than just simple "run of the mill" temptations. They were the terms for surrender. The encounter between Christ and Satan was a negotiation between the combatants before the battle resumed and intensified.

First, Lucifer attempted the same ploy used in the garden of Eden against Adam. Weakened and hungry from 40 days of fasting, Jesus was hungry (to use an understatement). His self-denial was not by choice. His Father had commanded His fast. The enemy invited Jesus to determine for Himself when He should eat. Ordinarily, choosing when one eats is not a sin, but for those who, like Jesus, are led by the Spirit, the Father's wish is their command. The choice was between self-determination and allowing God to determine for His Son what and when to eat.

In addition, Lucifer suggested that Jesus use powers no ordinary man could use. In either scenario, Jesus would have relied on Himself and His will rather than submitting to the will of His Father. Jesus said, "Man does not live by bread alone, but on every word that comes from the mouth of God." I will eat when my Father says so no matter how hungry I get or weak I feel. That is why the Word says He learned obedience through the things He suffered.

Next, knowing that Jesus would eventually have to confront the religious leadership, Lucifer suggests a grand entrance and introduction. He would throw Himself down from the highest point at the temple, and, like a death-defying daredevil, He would

---

24 Mark 9:2-8

escape unharmed with angelic aid. The Word promised that angels would protect Him.[25] There was only one problem, God had not told Him to perform such a stunt, and Jesus would not act or speak without His Father's express and specific instructions. To do otherwise would be testing the Lord. Again, the answer was "No!"

like David and Saul, two kings and two kingdoms are in deadly warfare for the same territorial realm

Finally, Lucifer came to the point. *I know why you are here. Only a flesh and blood man like Adam can retrieve what Adam lost. You came to get the scepter of power, to assume dominion and authority over all things. You came to be given the divine right to rule and reign You came to receive the kingdom. I'll tell you what I'll do for you. Rather than going through all of the acrimony and animosity, why don't we come to an accommodation? I'm not unreasonable. You don't have to go through any hardships or difficulties. Why suffer, why endure ridicule, scorn, reproach, suffering, beatings, and a horrible death? Let me offer you a shortcut and an easy way out. I will give you everything you came here to earth for in exchange for one little favor. Just bow down and worship me.*

"Get behind Me, Satan!" *First, the earth is the Lord's.*[26] *You have no kingdom to give. Whatever you think you have was usurped by manipulation, theft, and murder. Yet with all of that, it still isn't yours to give to anyone.*

Next, and most importantly, only God is to receive worship and Him only should one serve. I am completely yielded to my Father; and if I have to die to accomplish my assignment, so be it. As long as I live, I will do the will of Him who sent Me.

With that, the enemy left to regroup. He failed to trick the

25 Psalm 91:11
26 Psalm 24:1

Son of God out of His anointed position. Lucifer realized that the battle was on.

When David was anointed by Samuel to be king, Saul was still on the throne. In the wilderness, the prince of this world had just faced the king anointed by God to have authority and dominion over all things. Now, two kingdoms are in deadly warfare for the same territorial realm. Only one will ultimately reign. In the cace of Saul, he eventually died, and David took the throne. In Jesus' case, he began to demonstrate the benefits of God's kingdom immediately, and many began to force their way into it.

Chapter 4

The Kingdom Demonstrated

1 John 3:8

> He who does what is sinful is of the devil, because the devil has been sinning from the beginning. The reason the Son of God appeared was to destroy the devil's work.

Luke 11:14-20

> Jesus was driving out a demon that was mute. When the demon left, the man who had been mute spoke, and the crowd was amazed. But some of them said, "By Beelzebub, the prince of demons, he is driving out demons." Others tested him by asking for a sign from heaven. Jesus knew their thoughts and said to them: "Any kingdom divided against itself will be ruined, and a house divided against itself will fall. If Satan is divided against himself, how can his kingdom stand? I say this because you claim that I drive out demons by Beelzebub. Now if I drive out demons by Beelzebub, by whom do your followers drive them out? So then, they will be your judges. But if I drive out demons by the finger of God, then the kingdom of God has come to you.

Matthew 4:23-25, 10:1, 5-8

> Jesus went throughout Galilee, teaching in their synagogues, preaching the good news of the kingdom, and healing every disease and sickness among the people. News about him spread all over Syria, and people brought to him all who were ill with various diseases, those suffering severe pain, the demon-pos-

sessed, those having seizures, and the paralyzed, and he healed them. Large crowds from Galilee, the Decapolis, Jerusalem, Judea and the region across the Jordan followed him.

He called his twelve disciples to him and gave them authority to drive out evil spirits and to heal every disease and sickness.

These twelve Jesus sent out with the following instructions: "Do not go among the Gentiles or enter any town of the Samaritans. Go rather to the lost sheep of Israel. As you go, preach this message: 'The kingdom of heaven is near.' Heal the sick, raise the dead, cleanse those who have leprosy, drive out demons. Freely you have received, freely give.

Acts 8:4-8

Those who had been scattered preached the word wherever they went. Philip went down to a city in Samaria and proclaimed the Christ there. When the crowds heard Philip and saw the miraculous signs he did, they all paid close attention to what he said. With shrieks, evil spirits came out of many, and many paralytics and cripples were healed. So there was great joy in that city.

Matthew 5:43-48, 25:31-46

"You have heard that it was said, 'Love your neighbor and hate your enemy.' But I tell you: Love your enemies and pray for those who persecute you, that you may be sons of your Father in heaven. He causes his sun to rise on the evil and the good, and sends rain on the righteous and the unrighteous. If you love those who love you, what reward will you get? Are not even the tax collectors doing that? 47 And if you greet only your brothers, what are you doing more than others? Do not even pagans do that? Be perfect, therefore, as your heavenly Father is perfect.

"When the Son of Man comes in his glory, and all the angels with him, he will sit on his throne in heavenly glory. All the nations will be gathered before him, and he will separate the people one from another as a shepherd separates the sheep from the goats. He will put the sheep on his right and the goats on his left. "Then the King will say to those on his right, 'Come, you who are blessed by my Father; take your inheritance, the kingdom prepared for you since the creation of the world. For I was hungry and you gave me something to eat, I was thirsty and you gave me something to drink, I was a stranger and you invited me in, I needed clothes and you clothed me, I was sick and you looked after me, I was in prison and you came to visit me.' "Then the righteous will answer him, 'Lord, when did we see you hungry and feed you, or thirsty and give you something to drink? When did we see you a stranger and invite you in, or needing clothes and clothe you? When did we see you sick or in prison and go to visit you?' "The King will reply, 'I tell you the truth, whatever you did for one of the least of these brothers of mine, you did for me.' "Then he will say to those on his left, 'Depart from me, you who are cursed, into the eternal fire prepared for the devil and his angels. For I was hungry and you gave me nothing to eat, I was thirsty and you gave me nothing to drink, I was a stranger and you did not invite me in, I needed clothes and you did not clothe me, I was sick and in prison and you did not look after me.' "They also will answer, 'Lord, when did we see you hungry or thirsty or a stranger or needing clothes or sick or in prison, and did not help you?' "He will reply, 'I tell you the truth, whatever you did not do for one of the least of these, you did not do for me.' "Then they will go away to eternal punishment, but the righteous to eternal life."

John the Baptist, who announced that the "Kingdom of Heaven is near"[1] was in prison. It was this same John baptized Jesus, the Holy Ghost descended on Him in the form of a dove, and God the Father announced that "this is My Son, whom I love; with Him I am well pleased."[2] Now, in the solitude and isolation of Herod's prison, doubts began to swirl around in John's mind. He began to wonder about His cousin.[3] Was He really the Anointed One? He had heard about the growth of Jesus' ministry. so sent some of his disciples to ask Jesus if "He was the One or should we look for someone else?"

John knew that the kingdom was connected specifically to one individual. His assignment was to announce the arrival of that King and his kingdom. Even a prophet of John's caliber needed confirmation and reassuring. The most difficult work that is required of a believer is to believe the impossible, and often, implausible word revealed by God.[4]

Jesus sent John this word:

> Go back and report to John what you hear and see: The blind receive sight, the lame walk, those who have leprosy are cured, the deaf hear, the dead are raised, and the good news is preached to the poor.[5]

The kingdom of God was being manifested.

Jesus came to destroy the works of the devil and ultimately, to destroy him

After success in other regions of Galilee, early in His ministry,

---

1   Matthew 3:1-6
2   Matthew 3:13-17
3   Luke 1:36 stated that Mary and Elizabeth, John's mother, were related
4   John 6:28-29
5   Matthew 11:4-5

Jesus returned to his hometown of Nazareth. He chose the synagogue there to announce His anointing. He quoted Isaiah 61:1- 2 to describe what He was anointed to do as king.

> The Spirit of the Sovereign Lord is on me, because the Lord has anointed me to preach good news to the poor. He has sent me to bind up the brokenhearted, to proclaim freedom for the captives and release from darkness for the prisoners, to proclaim the year of the Lord's favor and the day of vengeance of our God, to comfort all who mourn,[6]

Notice that Jesus omitted the "day of vengeance" that was recorded in Isaiah's prophecy. For thousands of years, the inhabitants of the earth had been afflicted with and assaulted by the influences and effects of the dominion of darkness. Jesus came to destroy the works of the devil[7] and ultimately, to destroy him.[8] Sickness, oppression, bondage of all types and disease are all effects of the enemy's two main tools, sin and death. Jesus came not to condemn, but to set individuals free from Lucifer's control, influence, power and slavery.

One of the prevalent views of Jehovah in Jesus' time (and in some cases today) was that God was an exacting, mean, vengeful and tyrannical deity. Jesus' compassion, mingling with sinners, intolerance of hypocrisy, and love showed God in a light that had been obscured by religious tradition and flawed teaching passed down for centuries. The Father was in Christ reconciling the world unto Himself.[9] Jesus also came to reveal the Father to the world because as one looked, listened to and observed Him, they were seeing the Father.[10]

Authority Manifested

Everywhere that Jesus preached, taught and announced His

---

6   Luke 4:14-19
7   1 John 3:7-8
8   Matthew 25:41, Revelation 20:7-10
9   2 Corinthians 5:11-21
10 John 14:8-11

kingdom, the power that attended it was manifested. His authority went beyond His teaching. Sickness and disease obeyed His words. Demons begged for permission not to be sent to the abyss. Trees, winds, waves, and storm all responded to His commands. Laws of gravity were ignored as He walked and gave permission for Peter to walk on water showing what ordinary, flawed men might be able to do in Him. Thousands were fed with a young boy's sack lunch. Death itself, the primary weapon of fear wielded by Satan,[11] was not exempt from His jurisdiction. At His command the dead came back to life. He came to destroy the works of the devil, and He did just exactly that.

Once, after casting a demon out of man, Jesus was accused of using the power of Beelzebub (another name for the devil). Jesus responded that a kingdom divided against itself would not stand, but more importantly, if "I cast out demons with the finger of God then the kingdom has come unto you."[12] A part of what authenticated Jesus' ministry and message was the power of God that attended it. That power included absolute authority including authority over demons.

After He modeled His authority as the Anointed One and demonstrated the substance and power of His dominion for the 12 disciples and 70 others, He sent them out to preach and also to manifest its delivering power. They returned amazed that the demons were subject to them as they operated in Jesus' name.

Even after His departure the disciples, then called apostles, continued to preach the gospel of the kingdom with miracles, signs and wonders attending and confirming their ministries. Phillip, a Gentile deacon, had the same experience. Paul, who was not one of the original twelve, also had miracles, signs and wonders as an endorsement of his apostolic authority[13] as he also taught and proclaimed the Gospel of the Kingdom.

There were entire communities and regions where, once made aware of the presence of Jesus, or later His apostles, everyone who

11 Hebrews 2:14-15
12 Luke 11:14-22
13 2 Corinthians 12:12

was sick was brought to them and every single sick person was healed. Touching the hem of a garment, a handkerchief, or even allowing their shadow to fall on the infirmed person brought deliverance from sickness and the power of Satan.

The Transfiguration

A graphic example of the manifestation of the Kingdom of God is found in the events surrounding Peter's confession of Jesus being the Christ.[14] It all began with a simple question by Jesus. He asked, "Who do men say the son of man is?" The responses from his disciples ranged from Elijah, the most prominent and powerful of the Hebrew prophets, to John the Baptist, the recently martyred prophet.

He then gets to the point of His inquiry. "Who do you say that I am?" *You have shared what others have said about me. These are the statements of those who see me from a distance or once in a while. What I want to know is your impressions of me. You know me. You live with me. You travel with me. You eat with me. You see me up close and personal. We eat together. We sleep under the stars together. Who am I to you?*

Also, I know what you might say in My presence or under the peer pressure of the other disciples looking on, but what I want to hear is what you really think. What do you say to those you confide in? Who do you tell them that I am?

Silence fell on the men who had just freely spoken of the whispers and gossip of others about Jesus. They all looked at one another as if not knowing what to say or fearing to be the first to speak and get the answer wrong. Peter boldly stood to his feet and declared, "You are the Christ, the Son of the Living God."

Looking backward 2000 years, this appeared to be an easy confession to make, but it was a huge statement. It was saying that the Seed promised to Adam and Eve, the Prophet foretold by Moses, the Servant spoken of by Isaiah and the Prince prophesied by Ezekiel was standing in front of these men. Was this humble son of a carpenter from Nazareth the anointed King, descended

---

14 Matthew 16:13-17:9

from David and anticipated for centuries? Was this itinerant healer and teacher, who slept under the stars and, by His own admission, had no place to lay His head, the long awaited Messiah? The religious authorities, which were the very ones, one would imagine, to validate his claim, completely rejected Him. Now Peter, an ignorant fisherman with no formal theological training and a man prone to profanity, declared Him to be the Christ?

He did not look the part. He matched no one's image of royalty. He was despised and rejected of men. Some religious people labeled Him a sinner. He had no wealth, palace or possessions. How could He be the King anointed by God?

The flash of insight and fortitude to proclaim this was not natural. It was supernatural. It was a revelation from the Father that bypassed fear, questions, popular opinions and grasped faith. This revelation is the cornerstone upon which the foundation that the New Covenant church would be built. Nothing in this or any realm is stronger than His authority as King, including the gates of hell.

Those gates are like Gaza's gates in the hands of Samson[15] who singlehandedly ripped them from the walls and deposited them on a far away hill. A city's gate was one of the primary areas of defense protecting its inhabitants of the surrounding countryside from an invading army. The residents would flee to the safety of a walled city where they could defend themselves from a position of strength.

Gates also functioned to keep inhabitants in preventing their escape. It was also the seat of authority of the municipality. In warfare, if the gates of a city were breached, the city would be undefended and would certainly fall.

Peter's statement in Matthew that Jesus was the Christ, is the Rock upon which the Church is built and the gates of Hell cannot prevail against it.[16] The bastions of the enemy were defenseless against God's anointed King and His Authority.

Having received the response that He was looking for, He

---

15 Judges 16:1-3
16 Matthew 16:13-19

instructed His followers to keep this information to themselves, and began to reveal His coming suffering and death on the cross at the hands of His enemies the elders, chief priests and scribes. Peter, full of the pride of his prophetic revelation, presumes to tell Jesus what he would not allow Him to go through. Without realizing it, He allowed Satan to use him as an unwitting tool to revisit his final temptation offered to Jesus in the wilderness. He suggested that the redemption of the territory and descendants trapped by Adam's choice could be accomplished in some other way than the one prescribed by the Father. Jesus, however, was not fooled by the usurper's use of His brash disciple's voice, and His response is the same as it was in the wilderness, "Get behind me Satan!" I am the anointed King and I am still completely submitted to my Father in all things, even if it means suffering and death. Anyone who follows me will also follow my example and be prepared to lose his life for me too if necessary.

He concluded this exchange with a statement that has perplexed many. He said, "I tell you the truth, some who are standing here will not taste death before they see the son of man coming in his kingdom."[17] The kingdom, as has been previously explained, refers not to a church, organization, institution or even His second coming. He was referring to the visible manifestation of the revelation that came from Peter's mouth only a few moments before. It was a glance at the visible glory of His anointing as King that was cloaked in flesh and hidden from natural eyes.

Supernatural manifestation is not always a foolproof way to identify a God-ordained ministry

About one week after those words were spoken, Jesus took three of those who were part of the original conversation to a high mountain, out of the view of doubters, naysayers and skeptics.

17 Matthew 16:28

While he was praying,[18] His being was transformed into the true regalia of the Anointed One.

Each of the gospel writers point out the same characteristic: Light. His clothes and skin emanated the glory of His anointing expressed in the most brilliant light. It came from within Him and not from another source. Light so bright that it was brighter than the sun. As John put it, this was the glory of the only begotten of the Father.[19] He was (and is) Light — the true Light. Not reflected from some other source because He, Himself, is the source of all things, including light. These three saw the Christ unveiled in all of His splendor. They were privileged to see the King as He really was and as spirit beings and others in the universe saw Him. They saw the visible manifestation of the dominion of the anointed One invisible to the natural eye.

The Attributes of the Kingdom

Supernatural manifestation, however, is not always a foolproof way to identify a God-ordained and directed ministry. John the Baptist performed no miracles. Yet, based on Jesus' endorsement, he had no peer as a prophet.[20] His message and ministry were clearly sent by God.

The Egyptian wise men and Sorcerers did perform miracles.[21] A little slave girl could foretell the future by the power of an evil spirit.[22] The enemy can produce counterfeit signs, wonders and miracles.[23] Even Lucifer transformed himself into an angel of light.[24]

What separates those who operate in God's kingdom from those in the dominion of darkness is not the supernatural power manifested, but the attributes exhibited by the minister. Signs,

---

18 Luke 9:28
19 John 1:14
20 Matthew 11:1-15, John 10:40-42
21 Exodus 7:1-6, 22, 8:6-7
22 Acts 16:16-18
23 2 Thessalonians 2:9-10
24 2 Corinthians 11:14

wonders and miracles can be displayed and almost duplicated, but the Spirit of the Kingdom cannot.

What identifies the disciples of Christ and the sons of the Father is love. Sons of the Father love their friends and their enemies as well.[25] They bless those that curse them. They do good to those that hate them and pray for those that mistreat them.[26] Supernatural gifts can potentially be faked or misused, but the fruit produced by the Spirit of God cannot. This fruit, love, is how Jesus said that those connected to Him would be identified.

James and John, excited, yet immature in their understanding of the proper use of their power and privilege, suggested to Jesus that they call fire down from heaven to consume some unfriendly and inhospitable Samaritan towns. They were told that they had no idea what spirit was prompting that impulse.[27] They walked with Jesus, they saw his example and listened to His teaching. Yet, the spirit of condemnation, anger, vengeance and destruction from Satan was in them. As they were further mentored and trained, they came to understand that having power was good, but having the love that comes from knowing God and the indwelt Spirit of God was more essential. They would eventually learn the proper and appropriate use of their delegated authority. This is what would give evidence that they had the Spirit of God in them.

What identifies the disciples of Christ and the sons of the Father is love

Jesus also warned that many (not a few, but many) would preach, prophesy, drive out demons and perform mighty miracles in His Name; yet, they never knew Him. These are not counterfeit miracles. They are real, but done by individuals who do not know, or rather, are not known by the King of the kingdom for whom

25 Matthews 5:43-48, Luke 6:27
26 Luke 6:27-36
27 Luke 9:51-56 (margin)

they preached and performed supernatural wonders. They were called "workers of iniquity." They were giving aid and comfort to the enemy while supposedly serving and working for Christ.

The Spirit of God through Paul said, "the gifts and callings of God are without repentance."[28] This makes it possible for individuals to perform mighty and supernatural works in Jesus' name, yet be unsaved, operating in the flesh or unconnected in any way to the Spirit of His kingdom. Often, the inconsistency can confuse, complicate and bring condemnation on Christ. An example of this is when Moses got angry and struck the rock instead of speaking to it as he was commanded. God still performed the miracle. Moses, however, was dealt with severely for operating willfully out of his flesh (anger) instead of obeying God's voice.[29]

Somehow, however, souls are still saved, and the influence of the King advances in spite of the flaws, not only of the "workers" of iniquity, but also those who have weaknesses yet know and are known by the king. This is why Jesus warned the seventy, when they returned rejoicing victoriously that the demons were subject to them, not to revel in their newly discovered power and authority. Concern yourself not with supernatural power manifested in your ministry, but with He who has power to send ones' soul to hell and whether their names are written in the Lamb's book of life in heaven.[30]

Consistency with the Word

The Spirit of God, who distributes the gifts to men and women also is the Author of the scriptures. Someone who is manifesting the power of the Kingdom of God will also teach consistently with, rightly divide and operate personally and corporately in subjection to the Word of God, not in contradiction to it. They will confess that Jesus is Lord to the glory of God the Father. They will speak according to the scriptures. If they don't, it is because

28 Romans 11:29 KJV
29 Numbers 20:2-12
30 Luke 10:17-20

there is no light in them.[31]

Jesus exemplified both the power and the Spirit of His Kingdom. He did so, not only to set those free from the slavery and bondage of the enemy, but also to model for those delivered how to walk even as he walked. He predicted that there would be

those after Him who would do even greater works than He did.[32]

31 Isaiah 8:20 KJV
32 John 14:12-14

Chapter 5

Sons and Heirs of the Kingdom

John 1:10-18, 20:17

> He was in the world, and though the world was made through
> him, the world did not recognize him. He came to that which
> was his own, but his own did not receive him. Yet to all who
> received him, to those who believed in his name, he gave the
> right to become children of God— children born not of natural
> descent, nor of human decision or a husband's will, but born
> of God. The Word became flesh and made his dwelling among
> us. We have seen his glory, the glory of the One and Only, who
> came from the Father, full of grace and truth. John testifies
> concerning him. He cries out, saying, "This was he of whom I
> said, 'He who comes after me has surpassed me because he was
> before me.'" From the fullness of his grace we have all received
> one blessing after another. For the law was given through Mo-
> ses; grace and truth came through Jesus Christ. No one has
> ever seen God, but God the One and Only, who is at the Fa-
> ther's side, has made him known.

> Jesus said, "Do not hold on to me, for I have not yet returned
> to the Father. Go instead to my brothers and tell them, 'I am
> returning to my Father and your Father, to my God and your
> God.'"

Romans 8:13-17

> For if you live according to the sinful nature, you will die; but
> if by the Spirit you put to death the misdeeds of the body, you
> will live, because those who are led by the Spirit of God are
> sons of God. For you did not receive a spirit that makes you a

slave again to fear, but you received the Spirit of sonship. And by him we cry, "Abba, Father." The Spirit himself testifies with our spirit that we are God's children. Now if we are children, then we are heirs—heirs of God and co-heirs with Christ, if indeed we share in his sufferings in order that we may also share in his glory.

Genesis 1:26, 5:3

Then God said, "Let us make man in our image, in our likeness, and let them rule over the fish of the sea and the birds of the air, over the livestock, over all the earth, and over all the creatures that move along the ground."

When Adam had lived 130 years, he had a son in his own likeness, in his own image; and he named him Seth.

Galatians 3:26-4:7

You are all sons of God through faith in Christ Jesus, for all of you who were baptized into Christ have clothed yourselves with Christ. There is neither Jew nor Greek, slave nor free, male nor female, for you are all one in Christ Jesus. If you belong to Christ, then you are Abraham's seed, and heirs according to the promise. What I am saying is that as long as the heir is a child, he is no different from a slave, although he owns the whole estate. He is subject to guardians and trustees until the time set by his father. So also, when we were children, we were in slavery under the basic principles of the world. But when the time had fully come, God sent his Son, born of a woman, born under law, to redeem those under law, that we might receive the full rights of sons. Because you are sons, God sent the Spirit of his Son into our hearts, the Spirit who calls out, "Abba, Father." So you are no longer a slave, but a son; and since you are a son, God has made you also an heir.

1 Peter 2:9

But you are a chosen people, a royal priesthood, a holy nation, a people belonging to God, that you may declare the praises of him who called you out of darkness into his wonderful light.

Revelation 3:21, 1:6, 5:10 (KJV)

> To him who overcomes, I will give the right to sit with me on my throne, just as I overcame and sat down with my Father on his throne.

> And hath made us kings and priests unto God and his Father; to him be glory and dominion for ever and ever. Amen.

> And hast made us unto our God kings and priests: and we shall reign on the earth.

In John 12:24 Jesus revealed, in parable form, one of the purposes of His death. He said, "If a kernel of wheat falls to the ground and dies, it remains only a single seed. But if it dies, it produces many seeds."

The death of Christ accomplished many things for the believer. It paid the ransom, debt and wages of sin. It removed the guilt, condemnation, jurisdiction, sentence and penalty of the law. It also satisfied the wrath of God giving the one who walks by faith in Christ Jesus peace with Him.[1]

His death also opened the way for the sons of Adam to die by faith and sever the connection established when Adam yielded to the serpent and the dominion of darkness. Everyone born into this world is automatically a sinner. Because of Adam's sin, all men were made sinners, so men and women had no choice. Their actions and behavior resembled that of their father, the devil.[2] When Jesus died, however, He created the opportunity for a new and glorious life to everyone who would believe and receive it.

The Symbol of Death and Rebirth

When Jesus encountered Mary at the tomb after His resurrection and as He was trying to release Himself from her prolonged embrace, He said, "I am returning to My Father and your Father, to My God and your God." God was now Father to everyone who puts his or her faith and trust in Christ Jesus and, by that same faith, is now connected to Him. He is the first born of many brothers[3] (and sisters). Jesus gave men the option to choose to remain a son of Adam and the devil, or to be adopted as a son of God.

When an individual is baptized, this symbol of death, burial and rebirth into God's Kingdom is graphically demonstrated. First, the person is completely immersed in the water symbolizing the burial of a dead body. It is a public statement that by faith

---

1   This subject is explored in greater depth in The Father's Gift by S. Lloyd Walters Scepter Communications Inc. Altamonte Springs, FL 2006, 2016
2   John 8:42-47
3   Romans 8:29-30

in Christ that person has died. All that connected him or her to Adam, condemnation, etc. was severed.

The person is then raised up out of the water symbolizing that one's nature has been recreated with the Spirit of Christ implanted within by faith into a new birth and a new life. Nextthe believer accepts the reality, again by faith, that the Father has transferred the believer's connection to Christ instead of Adam as his or her head. Christ, Who pleases the Father and is seated at His right hand, is the Head of this new household of faith.

The life of Christ is miraculously and supernaturally deposited into the believer. Paul put it this way, "I have been crucified with Christ and I no longer live, but Christ lives in me."[4] The Father promised to put the Spirit of Christ in those who believe.[5] Therefore, Christ, by the Spirit of God, is now placed in the believer so that they can walk in a brand new life. They are now children, not of human will, but born of God.[6]

Remember that all of this is received by faith, which is an affirmative and active response to something that God has said. This means that the statements and declarations of God in the Word are believed and accepted without the benefit necessarily of any external evidence. In fact, evidence may seem to point in the opposite direction. Feelings, thoughts, circumstances, observations of friends or family, mistakes, shortcomings and weaknesses will argue that the word that the believer attached his faith to has not or will not come to pass. If one will patiently wait, however, believing that God will do what He said He will do, that individual will experience the manifestation of perhaps the greatest of all miracles – a life completely transformed from being a son (or daughter) of Adam, with all of the natural attributes and tendencies of the spirit of Lucifer, into a child of God. This has been attested to over and over again in the scriptures and in the lives of so many for centuries. Confess this often in prayer and believe it in one's heart and it will be manifested in one's life.[7]

---

4   Galatians 5:17-21
5   Romans 8:9-11
6   John 4:7-8
7   Roman 10:8-11

The one seed went into the ground and, when it sprouted, it created many seeds like the original seed. A single seed will produce fruit and grain, etc., but it will also produce more seeds. Those seeds in turn will produce still more fruit, grain, trees and flowers, but it will also, again, produce more seeds as well. The new seeds will produce yet more seeds, and on and on. Jesus' death was to reproduce Him many times over in the lives of His followers. These are not imitations, facsimiles or replicas. They are seeds like the first seed.

These sons walk like He walked and talk like the only begotten of the Father walked and talked. This is consistent with His prayer of John 17. He requested in His prayer to the Father that He himself would be in them that believe.[8]

The fruit of the Spirit, as mentioned in the previous chapter, shows the unmistakable evidence of a believer being in Christ: Love. Whoever loves, has been born of God and knows God.[9] Sons of God love like He loves. The Father lets the sun shine and the rain fall on the just as well as the unjust. He blesses those who curse Him and does good to those who do evil to Him. Perfection (or maturity)[10] is expressed in love. Prophecies, gifts, tongues and knowledge, while helpful and important to building up the body, do not produce what Jesus called being perfect. His Spirit makes the sons and daughters of God perfect in love. It is this same love one for another, Jesus says, that will identify all those who are His disciples. When that which is perfect (love) comes, everything else vanishes away.

The Rights of Sonship

There is however, another way that the sons of God look and act like Christ. In Galatians 3 and 4, the Spirit through Paul proclaims that those who were once enslaved, now through Christ they have been set free to receive the full rights as sons.

---

8   John 17:25-26
9   1 John 4:7-8
10 In more modern translations of the Bible the term "perfect" or "perfection" is rendered as being full grown or mature.

What exactly does these "full rights" mean and entitle us to?

In Jesus' parable of the two sons found in Luke 15 we get some insights into what it means to be a son. The younger of two sons, too impatient to wait for his father's death to receive his inheritance, demands that his father give it to him so he can live his life as he pleased. The father calculated the household estate and gave two thirds of the family wealth to the firstborn son and one-third to the younger son.

Due to his inexperience in the management of his resources, the younger son squandered his entire inheritance and found himself destitute. It should be noted that by demanding his inheritance while his father was still alive he disowned his family connection and was basically saying that his father was dead to him. His current destitute state, however, began to reorient his thinking. He swallowed his pride and started the journey back to his father's house.

As his wayward younger son returned home and with one third of the family's estate was gone because of this younger son's folly, one would expect a hostile reception to the wayward son's return. Yet, the father received him back with kisses, a robe, new shoes, a ring and a celebration.

Putting shoes on his younger son was an act of protection for the father. Only a slave goes barefoot. Being without shoes was considered a shame historically in Israel.[11] Whether deserved or not the father protected his son.

The father covered the younger son's tattered and soiled rags with a robe. The evidence of his sordid past was not to be seen by any curious onlookers. This is my son and nothing he has done is anyone's business. No matter how many indiscretions are in his past, I will cover them all. And all you need to see is this robe.

The ring, which may have been a signet ring bearing the family crest used to seal official transactions in the name of the father, was given to the younger son and was also probably worn by the older son. The signet ring is where we get the word signature, which is used to seal documents today. An example of a signet

11 Deuteronomy 25:5-10, Ruth 4:7-8

ring in those days was depicted in the film Ben Hur[12] starring Charleston Heston when Massala was wagering on the upcoming horse race and sealed the bet with the stamp of his ring on a wax tablet. Only mature sons, duly authorized to act in behalf of the father, could wear such a ring. By giving that ring to the younger son, the father vested his own authority on him, even before he proved himself worthy of the honor and responsibility.

Meanwhile, the older son, who remained home, refused to join in the celebration and remained outside in the field. The father went out and pleaded with him to join in the joyful festivities. The son complained that he had slaved for his father and "never transgressed any of his commandments."(KJV) Yet when this son of yours (because he rejected him as a brother) who wasted your money on prostitutes (as if he knew how his brother spent his inheritance, or perhaps revealing a hint of envy) came home, you put out the welcome mat and threw a party for him. I've served you and kept all of your commandments, but you have never given me anything."

The father gently corrected him, reminding him that he was always with him and everything that is his, he also owned. He also reminded and corrected him in respect to his relationship to his brother, no matter what he suspected that his younger sibling had done.

Based on this example, sons (and daughters) of a powerful and a loving father have certain rights. They have unlimited access to the father. Others may have to get an appointment or wait their turn to see him, but the father is excited and impatient to see his children. He might be the president of the United States, but to his children he is "Daddy." Even after his wayward son had strayed and soiled the family name, this father was anxious to receive his wayward boy back, personally.

Both sons received the generosity of the father. The younger son, who by right had forfeited any claim to anything that belonged to the father, was reinstated and was given access to the family's entire wealth. The older son, who spoke as if he was a hired hand,

---

12 Ben Hur Dir. William Wyler 1959 MGM. Film.

was reminded that he also had access to all that the father had. Nothing kept him from it except his own misconceptions and simply not taking advantage of what was already his.

There is a unique statement that Jesus makes in response to an inaccurate statement by Peter in Matthew 17:24-27:

> When they reached Capernaum, the collectors of the temple tax came to Peter and said, "Does your teacher not pay the temple tax?" He said, "Yes, he does." And when he came home, Jesus spoke of it first, asking, "What do you think, Simon? From whom do kings of the earth take toll or tribute? From their children or from others?" When Peter said, "From others," Jesus said to him, "Then the children are free. However, so that we do not give offense to them, go to the sea and cast a hook; take the first fish that comes up; and when you open its mouth, you will find a coin; take that and give it to them for you and me."

The question was about temple taxes but Jesus addressed king's taxes. He said that kings tax subjects not sons.

When Israel asked for a king, the prophet Samuel warned them that the king would require a tenth of their grain, vintage and flocks for his officials and attendants (see 1 Samuel 8). Melchizedek, king of Salem received a tenth of the spoils of war. Israelites, as subjects, were required to return a tithe (tenth) of the land and their flocks. Subjects are obligated to return a tenth to the king. This is the king's portion or the king's tax. All kings require that their subjects return a tenth of their increase from their realm. The sons of the king however, according to Jesus, are exempt from the king's taxes.

This is where many believers live. They are ignorant of the awesome rights and privileges that are theirs as sons. Often, this is because of the ignorance of those who lead congregations who, themselves, do not understand this gospel.

In his gentle words of reproof to his older son, the father was mildly disciplining his son. Every child can and should expect a father to discipline them. If he does not, one could question whether that father really loves that child or not.[13] This father clearly loved his sons and even in his pleading with them, he corrected and guided them.

All of these actions — access to the father, his generosity, protection, sharing his authority and discipline — stem from the depth of love that the father had for both sons. As a result of that love, the children who are the object of that love, have these and more as rights.

What love the Father has lavished on us that we should be called the children of God![14] Oh, that we could grasp how wide, and long and high and deep is the love of Christ! One thing should be kept in mind, that love is in His Son, Christ Jesus.

It is Jesus who pleased the Father. It is Jesus who always does the will of the Father. When Jesus was in the earth, He was in the Father and the Father was in Him. When Christ Jesus, by faith and through His Spirit, lives within the believer, that same love is showered on them.

The Spirit in Philippians explains the reason why the Father loves Jesus like he does. He humbled himself. Even though he had the status and rights not only of a Son, but also of being God, yet "He made himself nothing." He humbled Himself and became obedient even to the death of the cross.

God, His Father then exalted Him. With God, humility leads to promotion, exaltation, reward, favor and honor. When His sons humble themselves under His mighty hand, they are exalted in due time.[15] He gives grace (favor) to the humble.[16] With all of the rights available to Jesus, the anointed King, and the second Person of the Godhead, yet He yielded all of them to the will of His Father. For that God exalted Him. As a believer humbles himself under God's hand, He molds and fashions them according to His will. Then as His sons and daughters mature, God promotes them.

---

13 Hebrews 12:4-11
14 1 John 3:1
15 1 Peter 3:6
16 James 4:6

The Privileges of Sonship

As sons of God, by His Spirit, believers manifest the attributes of Christ in mind, body and spirit. The early disciples understood that meant that the works Jesus did, healing and performing miracles, they could and would do also. They even raised the dead. As sons of God, they not only had rights, but also certain privileges.

People would line the streets so that Peter's shadow would fall on them. Even his shadow was infused with his King's anointing.[17] During Paul's ministry, the handkerchiefs and aprons that he touched were taken to the sick and the demon possessed and all were healed.[18]

Supernatural manifestations are to be expected among the believers; they are sons and daughters of God. Jesus said that the Father promised them power and they were to walk and operate in that power. It confirmed their testimony and endorsed their teaching.[19] Deacons, like Phillip, preached and healed under the direction and power of the Holy Ghost.[20] Even his four daughters prophesied.[21]

As Jesus sent his disciples out to minister, He anointed and empowered them with authority just as the Father sent him. When they returned, they were amazed that even demons were subjected to them. Just before Jesus ascended to His Father, He said that all power and authority had been given unto Him.[22] This meant that through Him every believer had access to unlimited power and authority.

The Word of God declares that Jesus lives within the believer by the Spirit of God.[23] The body of the individual believer is the

---

17 Acts 5:12-16 Unusual manifestations of power did not only occur in the New Testament era. See also the miracles of Elijah and Elisha in 1 and 2 Kings.
18 Acts 19:11-12
19 Acts 14:3
20 Acts 8:4-8
21 Acts 21:8-9
22 Matthew 28:18-20
23 See Romans 8:9-11

temple of the Holy Ghost.[24] If Christ, the anointed King with all power and authority at His disposal, lives within, then nothing will be impossible for them by faith. This is why the believers of Paul's day saw and experienced "miracles, signs and wonders."[25]

Even the devils know this to be true. When the seven sons of Sceva tried to imitate the word and actions of Paul, the demons revealed that they knew the difference between those who had the endorsement of the Holy Ghost and those that were imposters. They punctuated their point with many punches and physical punishment.[26]

Salvation is a gift. Authority is earned

The earth groans for the appearance of the sons of God;[27] sons who walk and operate with the authority, power and Spirit of their Father. This is the enemy's worst nightmare. Men and women, boys and girls who, through their faith in God, walk in the knowledge that the Spirit of Christ lives within them will not only exhibit His fruit, but they walk in His power and authority. In a real sense, as believers operate in Christ's authority, they function as His body; an extension of His ministry on the Earth. The things that He did on the earth, they will do.

Submission

The key to operating in this authority is submission. Whoever humbles himself will be exalted.[28] Jesus submitted to the Father and was exalted and empowered. Submission to the authority of Father, Son and Holy Ghost is the prerequisite to being entrusted

---

24 1 Corinthians 3:16-17, 6:19-20
25 See 1 Corinthians 1:17,4:18-20
26 Acts 19:13-16
27 Romans 8:19-21
28 1 Peter 5:6, James 4:10

with authority. Those who pass that test will walk in that authority. Those who are proven untrustworthy and unfaithful, even what they have will be taken away.[29]

When believers operate in the fullness of their rights and privileges, they bring glory to the Father.

This is key to operating in power and authority. Jesus said, "I always do what I see the Father do and say what the Father wants me to say". One's content and conduct must align with God's purpose and will. Slvation is a gift. Authority, however, is earned. There are tests and training that must be successfully passed before one is given the reward. That is why many are called but few are chosen. And even some who are chosen can lose their exalted position, but yet be saved. It is interesting to note that Peter was sent to the Gentiles before Paul, but Peter could not rise above his bigoted upbringing. Both will be saved, but where Paul's role became enlarged, Peter's was diminished.

Coming Short of the Glory

Under the influence of the Spirit, John referred to the miracle of turning water into wine at Cana as Jesus revealing His glory.[30] When a son acts in a way pleasing to his father, he brings his father glory or praise. When believers operate in the fullness of their rights and privileges, they bring glory to the Father. Yes, all have sinned and come short of God's glory.[31] For those who are in Christ Jesus, however, all of their sins are forgiven. With the problem of sin dealt with, God's sons should be manifesting His

29 Luke 19:11-26, Matthew 21:41-44
30 John 2:11
31 Romans 3:23

glory; yet, this is the exception and not the rule. Why?

The subject of many sermons and, for that matter, the focal point of many ministries and churches is railing against sin. Whether it be homosexuality, promiscuity, lying, cheating, non-tithe paying, etc. this sin-focused emphasis keeps believers from experiencing victory and ultimately manifesting His glory. Sin-focused teaching and preaching tends to place the onus on the believer to make the necessary changes. It places the pressure on them to produce the behavioral results. This produces people who act the part in church and in front of others without any real transformation. This leads to hypocrisy and frustration and ultimately guilt and condemnation.

The gift that God gives us in Christ literally produces a new life in the believer; while at the same time eliminates guilt and condemnation. Look at what Paul writes:

> Now when a man works, his wages are not credited to him as a gift, but as an obligation. However, to the man who does not work but trusts God who justifies the wicked, his faith is credited as righteousness. David says the same thing when he speaks of the blessedness of the man to whom God credits righteousness apart from works: "Blessed are they whose transgressions are forgiven, whose sins are covered. Blessed is the man whose sin the Lord will never count against him."

> But thanks be to God that, though you used to be slaves to sin, you wholeheartedly obeyed the form of teaching to which you were entrusted. You have been set free from sin and have become slaves to righteousness.

> Therefore, if anyone is in Christ, he is a new creation; the old has gone, the new has come! All this is from God, who reconciled us to himself through Christ and gave us the ministry of reconciliation: that God was reconciling the world to himself in Christ, not counting men's sins against them. And he has committed to us the message of reconciliation. We are therefore

Christ's ambassadors, as though God were making his appeal through us. We implore you on Christ's behalf: Be reconciled to God. God made him who had no sin to be sin for us, so that in him we might become the righteousness of God.

Therefore, there is now no condemnation for those who are in Christ Jesus, because through Christ Jesus the law of the Spirit of life set me free from the law of sin and death.

You, however, are controlled not by the sinful nature but by the Spirit, if the Spirit of God lives in you. And if anyone does not have the Spirit of Christ, he does not belong to Christ. But if Christ is in you, your body is dead because of sin, yet your spirit is alive because of righteousness. And if the Spirit of him who raised Jesus from the dead is living in you, he who raised Christ from the dead will also give life to your mortal bodies through his Spirit, who lives in you.

Do you not know that the wicked will not inherit the kingdom of God? Do not be deceived: Neither the sexually immoral nor idolaters nor adulterers nor male prostitutes nor homosexual offenders nor thieves nor the greedy nor drunkards nor slanderers nor swindlers will inherit the kingdom of God. And that is what some of you were. But you were washed, you were sanctified, you were justified in the name of the Lord Jesus Christ and by the Spirit of our God.

At one time we too were foolish, disobedient, deceived and enslaved by all kinds of passions and pleasures. We lived in malice and envy, being hated and hating one another. But when the kindness and love of God our Savior appeared, he saved us, not because of righteous things we had done, but because of his mercy. He saved us through the washing of rebirth and renewal by the Holy Spirit, whom he poured out on us generously through Jesus Christ our Savior, so that, having been justified by his grace, we might become heirs having the hope of eternal life.

And we know that in all things God works for the good of those who love him, who have been called according to his purpose. For those God foreknew he also predestined to be conformed to the likeness of his Son, that he might be the firstborn among many brothers. And those he predestined, he also called; those he called, he also justified; those he justified, he also glorified. What, then, shall we say in response to this? If God is for us, who can be against us? He who did not spare his own Son, but gave him up for us all—how will he not also, along with him, graciously give us all things? Who will bring any charge against those whom God has chosen? It is God who justifies. Who is he that condemns? Christ Jesus, who died—more than that, who was raised to life—is at the right hand of God and is also interceding for us.

Romans 4:4-8, 6:17-18, 2 Corinthians 5:17-21, Romans 8:1-2, 9-11, Corinthians 6:9-11, Titus 3:3-7, Romans 8:28-34

The covenant of grace, known as the New Covenant, moves the focus from sin and condemnation to faith in Christ to forgive, justify, and produce righteousness in the believer. It is righteousness from God that is implanted in the believer by God. Again, Paul makes this point clear:

I have been crucified with Christ and I no longer live, but Christ lives in me. The life I live in the body, I live by faith in the Son of God, who loved me and gave himself for me. Galatians 2:20

The enemy's tactic is to tempt believers into acts of transgression to produce guilt and to shake their faith and confidence in their position in Christ. If we sin, we can confess our sin and we have an Advocate with the Father Who intercedes for us. We remain connected to Christ and are still sons.

> Therefore, brothers, since we have confidence to en-
> ter the Most Holy Place by the blood of Jesus, by a
> new and living way opened for us through the curtain,
> that is, his body, and since we have a great priest over
> the house of God, let us draw near to God with a sin-
> cere heart in full assurance of faith, having our hearts
> sprinkled to cleanse us from a guilty conscience and
> having our bodies washed with pure water. Let us hold
> unswervingly to the hope we profess, for he who prom-
> ised is faithful. Hebrews 10:19-23

When the focus centers continually on sin and related issues, walking in the authority of a son is both neglected and overlooked. Being perfect is not perfectionism. From a biblical perspective it is maturity born of the walk of the Spirit. What God provides is forgiveness and His Spirit within. This is what produces maturity.

The problem is many have not understood or been taught what it means to come short of the glory of God. Believers are now free to bring glory to God by walking and operating in this present world as sons and joint-heirs with His beloved Son and King. They can manifest His kingdom's power and authority right now.

At creation, God said let us make man after our image, after Our likeness. It was their intent to make a creature that would walk, speak, operate, rule and reign like its Creator. He made man ruler of all of the works of His hands, put everything under the man's feet, and made him and crowned him with glory and honor. Man lost all that.

In Christ, however, that has been restored so that now men, who were once children of the devil and by nature the objects of wrath,[32] can be called the sons of God with all of its rights and privileges. Every believer, from the least to the greatest, can exercise the authority that Christ did on the earth. Authority over sickness, disease, demons, and all of the other works of the enemy are collectively under their feet in Christ. The absence of this authority in believers is not a failure of God, but ignorance and unbelief of "Christians." Jesus said, His followers would do

---

32 Ephesians 2:3

greater things, if they believed.

Twelve disciples were in the boat, but only one walked on water, even though it was very brief. Because Peter dared to believe, ask, and attempt what he saw Jesus do, he did what Jesus did in spite of his many imperfections. Didn't Jesus say, that He only did what He saw His Father do?[33] So should every believer and every son of God.

Through Jesus, God is "Abba" (or Daddy). The height, width, breath, and depth of the love He has for His perfect, only Begotten Son, we come to know now, and the Holy Ghost sheds that love abroad in our hearts.[34]

Since believers are sons (and daughters), they are heirs and joint-heirs with Christ. By faith, they are seated with him in the heavenly realm at the right hand of God the Father.[35] Right now they are the Sons of God, reigning with Him while yet in hostile territory. Like Jesus did when He walked the earth, they respect the authority that exists here (police, governments, etc.) and exercise the authority that His kingdom has made available to them.

The single seed has become many seeds. And as these sons and daughters operate in their inheritance, they bring glory to God and his Christ, their elder Brother and King.

---

33 See John 5:19
34 Romans 5:5
35 Ephesians 1:20, Colossians 3:1, See Luke 22:69, Acts 2:33, 5:31, 7:56, Romans 8:34, Hebrews 1:13,10:12 and 12:2

Chapter 6

The Currency of the Kingdom

Matthew 14:13-21

> When Jesus heard what had happened, he withdrew by boat privately to a solitary place. Hearing of this, the crowds followed him on foot from the towns. When Jesus landed and saw a large crowd, he had compassion on them and healed their sick. As evening approached, the disciples came to him and said, "This is a remote place, and it's already getting late. Send the crowds away, so they can go to the villages and buy themselves some food." Jesus replied, "They do not need to go away. You give them something to eat." "We have here only five loaves of bread and two fish," they answered. "Bring them here to me," he said. And he directed the people to sit down on the grass. Taking the five loaves and the two fish and looking up to heaven, he gave thanks and broke the loaves. Then he gave them to the disciples, and the disciples gave them to the people. They all ate and were satisfied, and the disciples picked up twelve basketfuls of broken pieces that were left over. The number of those who ate was about five thousand men, besides women and children.

Acts 3:1-10

> One day Peter and John were going up to the temple at the time of prayer—at three in the afternoon. Now a man crippled from birth was being carried to the temple gate called Beautiful, where he was put every day to beg from those going into the temple courts. When he saw Peter and John about to enter,

he asked them for money. Peter looked straight at him, as did John. Then Peter said, "Look at us!" So the man gave them his attention, expecting to get something from them. Then Peter said, "Silver or gold I do not have, but what I have I give you. In the name of Jesus Christ of Nazareth, walk." Taking him by the right hand, he helped him up, and instantly the man's feet and ankles became strong. He jumped to his feet and began to walk. Then he went with them into the temple courts, walking and jumping, and praising God. When all the people saw him walking and praising God, they recognized him as the same man who used to sit begging at the temple gate called Beautiful, and they were filled with wonder and amazement at what had happened to him.

Matthew 6:19-34

"Do not store up for yourselves treasures on earth, where moth and rust destroy, and where thieves break in and steal. But store up for yourselves treasures in heaven, where moth and rust do not destroy, and where thieves do not break in and steal. For where your treasure is, there your heart will be also. "The eye is the lamp of the body. If your eyes are good, your whole body will be full of light. But if your eyes are bad, your whole body will be full of darkness. If then the light within you is darkness, how great is that darkness! "No one can serve two masters. Either he will hate the one and love the other, or he will be devoted to the one and despise the other. You cannot serve both God and Money. "Therefore I tell you, do not worry about your life, what you will eat or drink; or about your body, what you will wear. Is not life more important than food, and the body more important than clothes? Look at the birds of the air; they do not sow or reap or store away in barns, and yet your heavenly Father feeds them. Are you not much more valuable than they? Who of you by worrying can add a single hour to his life? "And why do you worry about clothes? See how the lilies of the field grow. They do not labor or spin. Yet I tell you that not even Solomon in all his splendor was dressed like one of these. If that is how God clothes the grass of the field, which is here today and tomorrow is thrown into the fire, will he not much more clothe you, O you of little faith? So do not worry, saying, 'What shall we eat?' or 'What shall we drink?' or 'What shall we wear?' For the pagans run after all these things, and your heavenly Father knows that you need them. But seek first his kingdom and his righteousness, and all these things will be given to you as well. Therefore do not worry about tomorrow, for tomorrow will worry about itself. Each day has enough trouble of its own.

Genesis 3:17-18, 8:21-22

To Adam he said, "Because you listened to your wife and ate from the tree about which I commanded you, 'You must not eat of it,' "Cursed is the ground because of you; through painful toil you will eat of it all the days of your life. It will produce thorns and thistles for you, and you will eat the plants of the field.

The Lord smelled the pleasing aroma and said in his heart: "Never again will I curse the ground because of man, even though every inclination of his heart is evil from childhood. And never again will I destroy all living creatures, as I have done. "As long as the earth endures, seedtime and harvest, cold and heat, summer and winter, day and night will never cease."

2 Corinthians 6:3-10

We put no stumbling block in anyone's path, so that our ministry will not be discredited. Rather, as servants of God we commend ourselves in every way: in great endurance; in troubles, hardships and distresses; in beatings, imprisonments and riots; in hard work, sleepless nights and hunger; in purity, understanding, patience and kindness; in the Holy Spirit and in sincere love; in truthful speech and in the power of God; with weapons of righteousness in the right hand and in the left; through glory and dishonor, bad report and good report; genuine, yet regarded as impostors; known, yet regarded as unknown; dying, and yet we live on; beaten, and yet not killed; sorrowful, yet always rejoicing; poor, yet making many rich; having nothing, and yet possessing everything.

Galatians 6:6-10

Anyone who receives instruction in the word must share all good things with his instructor. Do not be deceived: God cannot be mocked. A man reaps what he sows. The one who sows to please his sinful nature, from that nature will reap destruction; the one who sows to please the Spirit, from the Spirit will reap eternal life. Let us not become weary in doing good, for at the proper time we will reap a harvest if we do not give up. Therefore, as we have opportunity, let us do good to all people, especially to those who belong to the family of believers.

Matthew 17:24-27

After Jesus and his disciples arrived in Capernaum, the collectors of the two-drachma temple tax came to Peter and asked, "Doesn't your teacher pay the temple tax?" "Yes, he does," he replied. When Peter came into the house, Jesus was the first to speak. "What do you think, Simon?" he asked. "From whom do the kings of the earth collect duty and taxes—from their own children or from others?" "From others," Peter answered.

"Then the children are exempt," Jesus said to him. "But so that we may not cause offense, go to the lake and throw out your line. Take the first fish you catch; open its mouth and you will find a four-drachma coin. Take it and give it to them for my tax and yours."

Nehemiah 2:1-9

And it came to pass in the month Nisan, in the twentieth year of Artaxerxes the king, that wine was before him: and I took up the wine, and gave it unto the king. Now I had not been beforetime sad in his presence. Wherefore the king said unto me, Why is thy countenance sad, seeing thou art not sick? this is nothing else but sorrow of heart. Then I was very sore afraid, And said unto the king, Let the king live for ever: why should not my countenance be sad, when the city, the place of my fathers' sepulchres, lieth waste, and the gates thereof are consumed with fire? Then the king said unto me, For what dost thou make request? So I prayed to the God of heaven. And I said unto the king, If it please the king, and if thy servant have found favour in thy sight, that thou wouldest send me unto Judah, unto the city of my fathers' sepulchres, that I may build it. And the king said unto me, (the queen also sitting by him,) For how long shall thy journey be? and when wilt thou return? So it pleased the king to send me; and I set him a time. Moreover I said unto the king, If it please the king, let letters be given me to the governors beyond the river, that they may convey me over till I come into Judah; And a letter unto Asaph the keeper of the king's forest, that he may give me timber to make beams for the gates of the palace which appertained to the house, and for the wall of the city, and for the house that I shall enter into. And the king granted me, according to the good hand of my God upon me. Then I came to the governors beyond the river, and gave them the king's letters. Now the king had sent captains of the army and horsemen with me.

2 Corinthians 9:6-15

Remember this: Whoever sows sparingly will also reap sparingly, and whoever sows generously will also reap generously. Each man should give what he has decided in his heart to give, not reluctantly or under compulsion, for God loves a cheerful giver. And God is able to make all grace abound to you, so that in all things at all times, having all that you need, you will abound in every good work. As it is written: "He has scattered abroad his gifts to the poor; his righteousness endures forever." Now he who supplies seed to the sower and bread for food will also supply and increase your store of seed and will enlarge the harvest of your righteousness. You will be made rich in every way so that you can be generous on every occasion, and through us your generosity will result in thanksgiving to God. This service that you perform is not only supplying the needs of God's people but is also overflowing in many expressions of thanks to God. Because of the service by which you have proved yourselves, men will praise God for the obedience that accompanies your confession of the gospel of Christ, and for your generosity in sharing with them and with everyone else. And in their prayers for you their hearts will go out to you, because of the surpassing grace God has given you. Thanks be to God for his indescribable gift!

As Jesus was preparing His disciples for their first ministry trip without Him, He instructed them to, "take nothing for your journey: no staff, no bag, no bread, no money, no extra tunic." They were to exclude any provision that an ordinary traveler would take along on a trip to provide for their food and lodging. Imagine saying something like that to men who operated their own businesses and who collected taxes for a living at one time. Some of these men had families and responsibilities. There was no safety net, welfare, social security or unemployment insurance for their families at that time. That command would have raised more than eyebrows. How are they going to live and support themselves and their families?

In this world, as in the world of the disciples, it takes money to live. It takes money to be born. It takes money to go to school. It takes money to eat. It takes money (or at least the appearance of it) to get the girl and to keep her. It takes a lot of money to get married. It takes money to have children. It takes money to educate them. It takes money to maintain one's health. And if one should get sick, it takes money to get well or prolong life. It even takes money to die.

Jesus was introducing them to a currency that they had never heard of or utilized before

The pursuit of money merely to live is, by far, the most demanding and time consuming activity of all human endeavors. Even in areas where there is no legal tender, having items of value for barter or trade for the necessities of life occupy most, if not, all of an individual's waking hours. The lack of money can rob many of the remaining hours that was intended for sleep with anxiety, stress and worry. For some, the pressures of the loss of this all-encompassing means of exchange can lead to suicide.

By sending His disciples out without any cash, provisions and supplies, Jesus was introducing them to a currency that they had never heard of or utilized before. It was the currency upon which Jesus Himself lived. The disciples and soon to be apostles would, themselves, learn to live on this currency and teach their followers to do the same.

This currency of the kingdom is faith. It is not just faith in what you want or even need. It is faith in the One whom God has sent — faith in Christ. This is no vague concept or idea. This currency is more reliable than any other financial instrument or plan that has ever existed. Ultimately, believers will have to choose either to be controlled by the currency of this world (money) or the currency of the kingdom.

The Currency of this World

Jesus said, "You cannot serve God and money."[1] The pursuit of money to provide for legitimate needs of life is relentless and unyielding. Many work long hours or multiple jobs to provide for the basic needs of their families. The day begins, possibly before dawn, with a hastily swallowed meal then time spent in traffic or public transportation on to work. The day is spent often dealing with unpleasant co-workers or supervisors, but the need for the paycheck forces one to tolerate these unpleasantries. The evening comes and, after an equally unpleasant journey home and a hastily prepared meal, one rests only to repeat it all again four or five times or more throughout the week. By the weekend, fatigue and frustration has set in. If church and worship is to be included, it will be minimal, if at all.

In this scenario, the percentage of time and energy devoted to the pursuit of money dwarfs any and every other area of life. This pursuit is not for dishonest gain, nor is it for greed. It, for many, is just to meet life's basic needs. Some may put forth much more time and effort for "bigger barns,"[2] but many go through this type of struggle just to survive and subsist.

---

1   Matthew 6:24
2   See Luke 12:13-21

There is a prophecy in the book of Revelation that involves money.[3] It is the one that mentions the mark of the beast. Without going into whatever that mark of the beast may or may not be, the pressure exerted will be economic: not being able to buy or sell. Imagine not being able to buy gasoline, groceries or to pay rent or bills, etc. The role of money as a means of control and coercion is often used by the principalities of this world and is predicted in the Word. This begins to explain why Jesus purposely separated His disciples from the controlling, corrupting and manipulating influence of the spirit of mammon.

Money can be used to satisfy the lusts of the eyes and flesh as well as the pride of life, which all have their source in the world controlled by Lucifer. It can give a sense of security, power, status and importance. For many, even among Christians, having lots of money is a sign of favor and great faith, while the absence of it indicates being under a curse. Today money is now the measure of one's status in society. Whether in school, the workplace, or even at church, an individual is measured on the basis of what conspicuous evidence of wealth he or she displays. The world of music also exalts a wealthy lifestyle and its pleasures as the epitome of life in many of their promotional videos. This ironically makes the goal of the world and some in the church oddly similar. Too often, however, this display is merely a mirage simply to impress those looking on that a person is something, when in fact they have rented, borrowed or illegally appropriated their appearance of stature. In some places, the Gospel has been turned inward into selfishness and greed. The pursuit of wealth and increase has become the primary focus instead of the ability to command demons and releasing their captives from the bondage and infirmities of the dominion of darkness.

The Influence of Money in the Church

The apostles warned against those who were greedy for "filthy lucre."[4] They saw many examples of the power of corruption

---

3   Revelation 13:11-18
4   1 Timothy 3:3, 8 (KJV), Titus 1:7, 11, 1 Peter 5:5

that money could have. The apostles repeatedly cite the prophet Balaam, who sold his prophetic office for money, as a pattern to avoid.[5] Elisha's servant Gehazi, who lusted after silver and fancy clothes, is another prominent example.[6] Judas and others complained about the cost of the perfume and alabaster box presented to Jesus by a woman of ill repute, but only because of his greed. He also stole from the treasury.[7] A man tried to buy Holy Ghost power[8] and this greed and the love of money was part of the reason for Annanias and Saphira's death.[9]

there is another way to have one's needs met

This incident with Annanias and Saphira deserves a closer look. The actions of this husband and wife can be traced back to the generosity and sacrifice of all the believers and specifically of a Levite from Cyprus named Joseph, later called Barnabas. Annanias and Saphira observed, "no one claimed any of his possessions as his own, but they shared everything they had." They also noticed the notoriety that was given to Barnabas when he sold a field he owned and gave all of the proceeds to the apostles. They tried to pass off their gift as the same kind of sacrifice as Barnabas but could not bring themselves to give it all. Whether it was out of greed or need does not matter. They had their mind on the money and the money on their mind. They were entitled to give only a portion, but they wanted to impress men with a lie about money. It meant more than their integrity. God, who saw their heart, was not impressed.

---

5   See Genesis 22-25, Joshua 13:22, Jude 11, Revelation 2:14
6   See 2 Kings 5
7   John 12:4-6
8   Acts 8:18-24
9   See Acts 4:32-5:11

God's Approach to Meeting Man's Needs

According to Jesus, there is another way to have one's needs met and more. That is what He taught His disciples when He sent them out empty-handed. He said to seek first the Kingdom of God and His righteousness and whatever you need will be added to you. The kingdom, once again, is God's vesting of absolute authority over everything that He had created on His anointed Son, Christ Jesus. So, to seek the kingdom is to seek Him.

Abraham was told that God was his great reward.[10] The priests of the old covenant system had no inheritance because God said, "I am your inheritance."[11] Jesus told the devil, that man should not live by bread alone, but by every word that comes from the mouth of God.[12] Seek Me, He says and I will be your Source, your Provider, your Healer, your Righteousness, your Shepherd, your Peace, your Sanctifier, your Banner, your all and all.

Money can buy certain things, but Christ has power and authority beyond any amount of money. A believer that is connected to Him as a joint-heir gives him access to unlimited resources. In fact, the earth and everything in it is already His. As a joint-heir with Christ, the believer shares in the ownership of everything He possesses. An owner does not have to purchase what he already owns. Whether God will use miraculous means or the mundane method of money is up to Him. Yet, this is to be believed and received based solely on the Word of God without any visible evidence, which is the essence of faith. There is a popular saying that applies here:

This is the Word of God

I am what it says I am

I have what it says I have

I can do what it says I can do.

---

10 Genesis 15:1
11 Deuteronomy 18:1-2, Numbers 18:20, Joshua 13:14, 33
12 See Deuteronomy 8:3, Matthew 4:4

The currency of the kingdom, then is faith in what has God has revealed in His written and rhema word.

God's Methods of Increase

God's method of increase challenges the system and tendencies of the world and the flesh. A destitute prophet showed up at a widow's house. She was down to her last spoonful of meal and drop of oil. Yet, she was told to provide for the man of God first and afterward for her hungry son and herself. Most individuals in her position would throw the prophet out on his ear, yet when she obeyed, her faith in the word of God through the prophet was rewarded with an unending supply of meal and oil for the duration of the drought.

In Jesus' kingdom, one gives to get. Give, Jesus says and it will be given unto you.[13] One's generosity in giving will determine how generous one will receive.

The tithes of the old covenant, or tenth, is really the king's portion.[14] In this system, the king's officials and servants were supported by a tithe of that land, of the grain of the soil, or fruit of the tree. The new covenant replaces the old. So what became of the tithing system?

Jesus shocked the rich young ruler when He told him to "sell all he had and give to the poor."[15] That far superseded the tenth and the ruler was unprepared for that level of giving. In essence Jesus expanded the boundaries of giving beyond ten percent to whatever the king requested.

Abraham, who lived before the old covenant era, paid tithe to Melchizedek.[16] The tithe was, in affect the king's portion (or his tax). When God demanded a tenth and when Abraham gave

---

13 Luke 6:37 Even though this passage is about judging and condemnation, the underlying principle can be applied to whatever one gives. Other scriptures further support this principle as well (see 2 Corinthians 9:6-11 and Galatians 6:7-10).
14 See 1 Samuel 8:15-17, Genesis 14:17-20
15 Luke 18:18-29
16 Genesis 14:17-20

a tenth to Melchizedek the principle of the king's portion was being applied.[17] Jesus, however stated that kings tax subjects and not sons. In fact He stated that sons are exempt.[18] Giving, then under the new covenant is different than the old.

The era of giving based on rules ended with the Old Covenant. Now the believer listens to the voice of God for instructions regarding his giving will often, if not always exceed Old Covenant giving.

With God to win, often, one would have to lose

To whom one gives is also important. The wise man, Solomon, wrote. He that is kind to the poor lends to the Lord.[19] According to the prophet Ezekiel of the Old Testament, among the reasons for the destruction of Sodom was the callous and careless treatment of the poor, the fatherless and the widows.[20] Notice that Israel was consistently instructed direct their collective giving and to provide food storehouses for the Levites, the fatherless, widows and foreigners.[21] The blessing of God pursued those who cared for those who had the least.

With God to win, often, one would have to lose. If someone takes your coat, give him or her your cloak too, Jesus said. Going the extra mile would be rewarded in His Kingdom.[22] He went as far as suggesting that one should give without expecting repayment.[23]

Weakness was preferred to strength in God's strategy. He never chose superior numbers or strength to accomplish His will.

---

17 See 1 Samuel with special emphasis on verses 8-17 as Israel asks for a king.
18 See Matthew 17:24-27
19 Proverbs 19:17
20 Ezekiel 17:49-50
21 Deuteronomy 24:19-21, 26:12-13, Psalm 146:9, See Ezekiel 27:7
22 Matthew 5:38-42, Luke 6:27-36
23 Luke 6:29-30

He gave Gideon 300 men to defeat 135,000.[24] A teenager, David, defeated a seasoned giant of a warrior, Goliath.[25] He chose 12 unlearned men to reach the world. He fed thousands with a sack lunch.[26]

David wrote that no king is saved by the size of his army.[27] No warrior escapes by his great strength.[28] He also wrote that some trust in chariots and some in horses, but we will trust in the name of the Lord our God.[29] This is one of the reasons why God dealt so severely with him when he numbered the fighting men of Israel as if superior numbers would ensure victory against an enemy instead of trusting in God.[30]

God is glorified when His people are outnumbered, over matched and backs are against the wall. He said, "My strength is made perfect in weakness.[31] I've chosen the foolishness of this world to confound the wise;[32] the despised things and things that are not confound things that are". Anyone can defeat a Pharaoh with an overwhelming army, but God said sent old men and a stick, some flies, gnats, hail, darkness, etc. and brought the most powerful nation of its day, Egypt, to its knees.[33]

"When I sent you out without purse, bag or sandals, did you lack anything?" Jesus asked His disciples. They answered "Nothing."[34] The currency of this kingdom, faith in His Word, is more spendable and reliable than anything that the world system can offer.

The size of one's bank account often is viewed as an indication of how blessed by God one is. In fact, there are examples in the

---

24 Judges 7:1-8:21
25 1 Samuel 17
26 John 6:1-13
27 Psalm 33:16-19
28 Ibid
29 Psalm 20:7
30 1 Chronicles 21
31 2 Corinthians 12:7-10
32 1 Corinthians 1:18-31
33 Exodus 5-15
34 Luke 22:35

word that suggest that material wealth came to those who were faithful to God: Abraham, Job, Solomon, etc. There are those today who have arrived at their wealth the same way these great men of old did and are using it to be a blessing to others and, even more importantly, to support the proclamation of the kingdom.

Yet, James places the man of humble means in a high estate and the wealthy man in a low estate, because wealth can evaporate like water on a sidewalk in the noonday sun (or like dot com stocks).[35] The apostle Peter, a former business owner, says to a lame man "Silver and gold I do not have, but what I have, I give you."[36] The currency he had was not a platinum American Express Credit Card (or its contemporary equivalent), it was faith. Faith that could appropriate for that man some legs that would walk run and leap for joy. That is something money could not buy.

Nehemiah was the cupbearer of the king, but he was visibly upset. The King noticed his servant's downcast disposition and inquired what was wrong. Nehemiah informed the king about his concern for the unrepaired walls of Jerusalem. The king asked one question, "What do you want?" With prayerful boldness Nehemiah told the king the desires of his heart. The king did not give him money. He provided this humble cupbearer official correspondence to the provincial governors signed and sealed by the king giving him access and authority over the kingdoms vast resources. He also dispatched troops to accompany Nehemiah to protect and further validate his bona fides on his way.

This currency of the kingdom may not necessarily translate into money. In fact, Paul warns Timothy against those who "think godliness is a means to financial gain", and "lovers of money."[37] They were using the gospel as a "get rich quick" scheme. God was being pursued as a means to great wealth and possessions. He was a genie that would provide what one wanted if one said the right things and rubbed Him the right way. It is interesting to note the violent reaction of Christ Jesus to the temple being transformed

---

35 See James 2:5-7
36 Acts 3:1-10
37 1 Timothy 6:3-10

place of merchandising and a "den of thieves."[38] Paul said "People who want to get rich fall into temptation and a trap and into many foolish and harmful desires that plunge men into ruin and destruction."

Covetousness verses Contentment

The root of all sin is covetousness. Covetousness is to desire for that which one is not rightfully entitled to or belongs to someone else. The sin of adultery, for example, begins with desiring a woman (or man) that belongs to another.

Contentment, however as described by Paul, is the polar opposite of covetousness. He said whatever state one finds oneself, whether in humble circumstances or in plenty, one is to be content. The believer is to learn to be content with the necessities of life for "godliness with contentment is great gain."

This same apostle, in describing his hardships, said he was poor, yet was making many rich, having nothing, yet possessing everything.[39] He, from the natural eye, had nothing, but with the eye of the Spirit, possessed all that his joint-heir, Christ had — Everything. He said that he knew how to be in need and how to have plenty. The secret is to be content in every situation knowing that through Christ he could do all things.[40]

Under the Old Covenant all of the tribes received an inheritance of land except the tribe of Levi. They ministered in the temple in the presence of the Lord. Over and over again the God of Abraham reminded them that, "I am your inheritance."[41] To some, this would appear to be a slight and a raw deal, but it is like having access to the owner of the bank rather than simply having an account in that bank. The Lord declared in effect, *I am the source of all things, so if one has Me, he will possess everything.* That was the blessing of serving in the presence of God under the Old Covenant. In the New Covenant every believer is not only a

---

38 Matthew 21:12-13
39 2 Corinthians 6:3-10
40 Philippians 4:12-13
41 See Deuteronomy 18:1-2, Numbers 18:20, Joshua 13:22, 33

priest in His presence, but also a son and a king entitled to every benefit that comes with it: health instead of a health care plan and miraculous provisions instead of a few pennies.

This cannot be overemphasized. Jesus made the distinction between subjects and sons. As heirs we are seated with Him in heavenly places. All that He has is ours. Anytime our Father decides to release it to us, He can, and in any way He chooses to. Often, it is not how we expect or by conventional means. He might use five loaves and two fish or plain water in some jugs. How he chooses to provide for his children is entirely in His hands, and he will do it in a way that it is clear that He did it and no one else so that all of the glory goes to Him

Principles of Increase

There are some principles in the Word regarding increase and the currency of His Kingdom. First, the believer is commanded to work. The all-powerful Creator of the universe called the activity of creation "work."[42] He set the example for His son, Adam. In fact, one of the assignments for Adam was to care for the Garden of Eden because "there was no man to work the ground."[43]

Believers are to work like the Father works. Whatever their hands find to do, they are to do with all of their might.[44] Paul even suggested that if a man does not work, he should not eat.[45]

The work that one is to do may vary according to one's respective gifts, abilities and opportunities. Whether the job is mopping a floor, driving a truck, teaching a class, arguing a case, preaching a sermon or writing a book, it is to be done with diligence and wholeheartedly as unto the Lord,[46] knowing that He is the One who gives the power to get wealth.[47] The results of labor

---

42 Hebrews 4:3
43 Genesis 2:4-5
44 Ecclesiastes 9:10a
45 2 Thessalonians 3:10
46 Ephesians 6:7-8
47 Deuteronomy 8:18 (KJV)

and all increase still rests in His hands.

God also modeled rest from labor by instituting the Sabbath at the end of the creation week. This weekly 24-hour cessation from work provided for the physical, emotional, mental and spiritual rejuvenation of man. The Sabbath was a shadow of the deeper spiritual rest experienced by the New Covenant believer who depend totally on God as the author and finisher of every aspect of his faith. In other words, man's complete rest and well-being is found, not in a day, but in faith in Christ. He said,

> Come unto me, all ye that labour and are heavy laden, and I will give you rest. Take my yoke upon you, and learn of me; for I am meek and lowly in heart: and ye shall find rest unto your souls. For my yoke is easy, and my burden is light. Matthew 11:28-30 KJV

The rest that man seeks is found in Christ because those "who believe enter that rest."[48]

The work of the apostle, prophet, evangelist and pastor / teacher is no less demanding, even though it may appear to be. The work of prayer and the ministry of the Word was so important to the apostles that the legitimate needs of the Gentile widows could not be allowed to distract them. Wrestling with the Word and persevering and interceding in prayer would sometimes include days of fasting and isolation with the Author of all things. While to some it looks like easy work, for those who have been called and make the ministry of the word and prayer their full time responsibility each should be respected and generously remunerated. Those who, like Paul, also work with their hands[49] should also be respected and also rewarded for their labor.

Rewards

Another principle of the currency of the kingdom is that of rewards. In Matthew chapter 6 Jesus described three things done secretly: giving to the needy, praying and fasting. These are done

---

48 Hebrews 4:1-11
49 1 Corinthians 4:12, 9:6

out of the view of other so as not to be noticed, yet the Father, Who observes what was done quietly and out of the public eye, will generously reward openly. He says that those that do these things to be seen of men have already received their reward (accolades and the praise of men). However, if these things are done secretly, so that only God knows what was done, the believer will be rewarded openly.

There is a profound difference between salvation and rewards. We are all saved by grace. Nothing that we do or will do can earn any aspect of salvation.

However, Jesus said that many are called but few are chosen. One can be the least in the Kingdom. These statements do not refer to salvation but promotion and reward. The greater the responsibility one has in His Kingdom, the greater the reward. Rewards then have to do with faithfulness after salvation. It has to do with being eligible for honor and promotion once one enters the Kingdom of God.

32,000 Israelites answered Gideon's call to arms, but ultimately only 300 were honored with the victory.[50] All were still covenant sons of Abraham, but only 300 were honored above their fellow.

The mother of James and John requested that her sons be seated at the right and left hand of Jesus. There were some requirements that went with that honor — to drink of the cup that Jesus would drink.[51] The reward is given to those who are willing to yield, obey, be broken, deny self, mortify the flesh, take up one's cross and follow Christ.

Blessing God's Servants

There were also rewards for those who show kindness and generosity to those whom He has sent.

> He who receives you receives me, and he who receives
> me receives the one who sent me. Anyone who receives
> a prophet because he is a prophet will receive a proph-

---

50 Judges 7:1-8:21
51 Matthew 20:20-28

et's reward, and anyone who receives a righteous man because he is a righteous man will receive a righteous man's reward. And if anyone gives even a cup of cold water to one of these little ones because he is my disciple, I tell you the truth, he will certainly not lose his reward.[52]

What are these rewards? For a widow in Zarephath, it was a continual miraculous supply of flour and oil for the duration of the drought and the resurrection of her son;[53] for another widow it was miraculous debt elimination;[54] for the Shunammite woman it was the miraculous birth and resurrection of her son and restoration of her land and income.[55]

God told Abram as he returned from routing four kings with 318 men that he was his shield and his very great reward.[56] Abram, in faith, went to battle to rescue his nephew, Lot and his family, believing that the God who called him would also protect him. He was not only Abram's protector and defense, but He was also a reward greater than money, greater than the spoils of war, greater than real estate, greater than honor, greater than fame or anything else that a man could desire. The prophet's reward is having God Himself as a confidant, friend and benefactor.

God supplies all seed

Today, God's Spirit dwells in the body temples of His recreated sons and daughters. His Word is proclaimed by servants of El Elyon (the Most High God). Those who, in obedience to the Spirit of God, assist His servants like these women did Elijah, Elisha and women helping to support Jesus' ministry out of their own means,[57] will also see God reward them.

---

52 Matthew 10:40-42
53 1 Kings 17:7-24
54 2 Kings 4:1-7
55 2 Kings 4:8-37, 8:1-6
56 See Genesis 14
57 Luke 8:1-3

Sowing and Reaping

When a farmer sows seed, he expects a harvest. This is another important principle in the Kingdom: seedtime and harvest. Before God created man, He made "seed-bearing plants and trees." That theme was continued even within man. Plants, trees, fruit and even man had seed within itself, enabling them to reproduce themselves many times over.

There are many types of seed in the Word. Jesus is referred to as a seed.[58] The word of the kingdom is also called seed.[59] Resurrected saints and sons of the Kingdom are called seed in parables as well.[60] Money and gifts are referred to as seed also.[61]

God supplies all seed. Whether of the plant variety or money; He sees to it that everyone has some kind of seed. As one sows that seed, they can expect a harvest proportionate to the seed sown. If one sows only a few seeds, he cannot expect a large harvest. Whatever a man sows, that is what he will reap. Even if that seed is an investment in time, kindness, prayer, faithfulness or if it is hate, malice, lust, etc. the principle of seedtime and harvest will always apply.

The believer has access to a new currency

Any farmer will tell you that there is a waiting time between when one plants the seed and the harvest. It is not immediate or instantaneous, even though some plants grow faster than others. The distance between the seasons of seedtime and harvest in the Jewish calendar is six months, so sowing is followed at times by periods of waiting. That is why it is advisable to sow all of the time.

---

58 John 12:24
59 Matthew 13:19
60 Matthew 13:38, 1 Corinthians 15:35-44
61 2 Corinthians 9:6-15

Again, all of this is believed and received by faith. This faith must be based on the Word of God and not anything else. The one that believes the Word also confesses or speaks it aloud. They, like their heavenly Father, speak things that are not as though they are[62] and their faith in Christ Jesus is ultimately rewarded.

As believers apply these principles of work, rewards, and seedtime and harvest, they will be activating the principles that create real wealth. Even for those who are not believers, if they utilize these principles, they will and do experience increase.

The believer, however, has access to a new currency. This currency provides supernatural benefits. One that does not have to be seen to be experienced or realized. That currency is their inheritance in Christ by faith. He Himself is that currency. This currency does not fluctuate with the market. It is not in a bank where thieves break in and steal. Faith in Him is the currency of the kingdom.

---

62 Romans 4:17

Chapter 7

Finding the Kingdom

Matthew 13:44-46

"The kingdom of heaven is like treasure hidden in a field. When a man found it, he hid it again, and then in his joy went and sold all he had and bought that field. "Again, the kingdom of heaven is like a merchant looking for fine pearls. When he found one of great value, he went away and sold everything he had and bought it.

Luke 18:18-30

A certain ruler asked him, "Good teacher, what must I do to inherit eternal life?" "Why do you call me good?" Jesus answered. "No one is good—except God alone. You know the commandments: 'Do not commit adultery, do not murder, do not steal, do not give false testimony, honor your father and mother.'" "All these I have kept since I was a boy," he said. When Jesus heard this, he said to him, "You still lack one thing. Sell everything you have and give to the poor, and you will have treasure in heaven. Then come, follow me." When he heard this, he became very sad, because he was a man of great wealth. Jesus looked at him and said, "How hard it is for the rich to enter the kingdom of God! Indeed, it is easier for a camel to go through the eye of a needle than for a rich man to enter the kingdom of God." Those who heard this asked, "Who then can be saved?" Jesus replied, "What is impossible with men is possible with God." Peter said to him, "We have left all we had to follow you!" "I tell you the truth," Jesus said to them, "no one who has left home or wife or brothers or parents or children for the sake of the kingdom of God will fail to receive many times as much in this age and, in the age to come, eternal life."

Genesis 49:10

The scepter will not depart from Judah, nor the ruler's staff from between his feet, until he comes to whom it belongs and the obedience of the nations is his.

As mentioned earlier, the coming Kingdom of God and its anointed One was a passionate hope of all Israelites including the disciples. Even after 40 days of instruction about the Kingdom, they were still anticipating the political restoration of the supremacy of Israel over all of the nations of the earth with the Prince on the throne of David.[1]

Jesus informed them that it was not for them to know the times and the seasons.[2] Today, however, with the benefit of the writings of the prophets and the apostles, one can see the unfolding of the mystery of God's will to bring all things in heaven and earth together under one Head, Christ.[3]

Jacob, who was also known as Israel, prophesied that, "The scepter will not depart from Judah, nor the ruler's staff from between his feet, until he comes to whom it belongs and the obedience of the nations is his."[4] This prophetic scepter, a rod or stick held by a king or a queen as a sign of royal power and authority, symbolizes the rule and reign of Christ. Metaphorically, this scepter was originally handed to Adam, who proved unworthy to hold it. Since then this king's rod has been waiting for millennia for someone worthy to take possession of it.

This has been God's primary purpose throughout Earth's history — to bring everything and all authority under one head, even Christ.[5] This was why John the Revelator wept when no one could be found to take hold of the scroll, and heaven rejoiced when the Lamb that was slain finally stepped forth to retrieve it.[6] This was prophesied long before He came.[7] His birth was heralded as the arrival of this anointed King.[8] He now has all authority in Heaven and in Earth.[9] The final subjugation of the

---

1   See Ezekiel 37:15-28
2   Acts 1:6-7
3   Ephesians 1:3-10
4   Genesis 49:10
5   Ephesians 1:3-10
6   Revelation 5
7   Genesis 49:10, Psalm 2:9, Isaiah 9:6-7
8   Luke 1:26-38, 2:8-20
9   Matthew 28:18-20

dominion of darkness is yet to come.[10]

The prophecies of Daniel focused on the arrival of the Kingdom of God and its ultimate destruction of the kingdoms of this world.[11] The King and his coming Kingdom is a major emphasis of the whole Bible, but especially for the Hebrew prophets as Israel was warned about and then forced into exile.[12] The fact that their nation and people had been subject to occupation by the Babylonian, Medo-Persian, Greek and Roman empires only heightened their desire for a political deliverer like Moses had been during Israel's enslavement in Egypt. It is no surprise that the focus of every Jew of Jesus' day was looking for the coming of God's anointed king.[13]

They were looking for the Messiah. It is important to note that the term "Messiah" and "Christ" both mean the same thing; The Anointed One. The only difference is that the term "Messiah" is the Hebrew translation and "Christ" is the Greek translation of the same term. They both refer to the Anointed Son of David who was to come and reign on his throne.

How, then could they miss His arrival? John the Baptist announced His coming. Jesus Himself preached it and confirmed it with miraculous signs. Yet many, including the various religious communities and leaders, not only rejected him as king, but also were instrumental in His unjust trial and execution.

When Jesus was born, it was priestly mystics from the East, not from Jerusalem or the temple that welcomed His birth with gifts and worship. Shepherds were informed by celebrating angels that the Christ was born. What the Apostle Paul calls the mystery of Christ was hidden from the wise, but revealed to the simple by the Spirit of God.[14]

Only five times in the gospels did Jesus plainly state who He

---

10 See Psalm 2; 45; 110; Revelation 12:5; 19:11-15
11 See Daniel 2
12 Jeremiah 25
13 Acts 1:6
14 See 1 Corinthians 1:18-31, 2:6-16, Ephesians 3:2-13

is. He told Peter,[15] the woman at the well,[16] the man who was born blind,[17] the high priest Caiphas[18] and Pilate in response to a direct question.[19] The only time that anyone was allowed to see the King's majesty was on a mountaintop far from Jerusalem.

This King was the opposite of any king they had ever seen.

Jesus told His disciples after being asked why He spoke to the people in parables because

> "The knowledge of the secrets of the kingdom of heaven has been given to you, but not to them. Whoever has will be given more, and he will have in abundance. Whoever does not have, even what he has will be taken from him. This is why I speak to them in parables: "Though seeing, they do not see; though hearing, they do not hear or understand. In them is fulfilled the prophecy of Isaiah: "'You will be ever hearing but never understanding; you will be ever seeing but never perceiving. For this people's heart has become calloused; they hardly hear with their ears, and they have closed their eyes. Otherwise they might see with their eyes, hear with their ears, understand with their hearts and turn, and I would heal them.' But blessed are your eyes because they see, and your ears because they hear. For I tell you the truth, many prophets and righteous men longed to see what you see but did not see it, and to hear what you hear but did not hear it.[20]

Those who have ears to hear and eyes to see, meaning ears and eyes activated by the Spirit of God and the Word, would grasp

---

15 Matthew 16:13-20
16 John 4:25-26
17 John 9:35-38
18 Matthew 26:63-64
19 John 18:33-37
20 Matthew 13:11-18

and understand the kingdom.

A Different King

Normally, kings look and act a certain way. They have great wealth and command impressive and intimidating armies. They are arrayed in fine clothes and live in palatial palaces. This King however was the opposite of any king they had ever seen.

He did not muster an army around Him. He did not enlist the assistance of the leading political and religious leaders. His followers ranged from prostitutes to foul-mouthed fishermen; from collaborators with Rome to insurgents. His rhetoric about loving your enemies[21] confused his followers who longed for a deliverer form Roman oppression. He chose to use obscure and vague parables to inform them and the multitudes about the nature of His Kingdom.[22]

The parable of the sower is about the kingdom; the seed is the message of the kingdom. Some allow Satan to take the message from their hearts by misunderstanding or misrepresentation. Others allow trouble, persecution, worries of life, or the deceitfulness of wealth to make it wither or choke the life out of it. Then, there are those who understand it, receive it by faith and are subsequently fruitful;[23] fruitful in their lives, families, ministries, and in many other ways.

Sold Out

The gospel of the kingdom is received individually by revelation by the Spirit of God. He said you would find Me if you would seek Me with all of your heart.[24] He also said to ask, knock and seek, because everyone who did would be given unto, the door would be opened, and find what was sought would be found.

When Peter proclaimed that Jesus was the Christ, He said

---

21 Matthew 5:43-44
22 See Matthew 13:10-17
23 Matthew 13:1-9, 18-23
24 See Jeremiah 29:13

that the Holy Ghost revealed Peter's outburst to him,[25] and the impact of discovering and understanding what this revelation can have on one's life is profound. Jesus described what happens when one finds it by describing two men.

The first one stumbled upon a great treasure as he walked across a field. He rushed home and liquidated all he could get his hands on and bought the entire field. The other man was a merchant of fine pearls. He happened upon the most precious and priceless pearl that his experienced eyes had ever seen. He, like the first man, sold all that he had and purchased the pearl.

Both men sold out completely just to acquire the object they considered to be of the most supreme value. What Jesus was saying was that the discovery of the kingdom of God, the rule and reign of God's anointed king, is of such value that men would sell out completely for it.

A rich young ruler came to ask Jesus about how one can receive eternal life. After listening to his boasts about observing the commandments, Jesus suggested that he sell all he had and follow Him. Jesus was actually telling him to sell everything and pursue Him as his king. In doing so he would be entering into eternal life and the kingdom of God. Notice once again that Jesus puts aside the ten percent standard of the old covenant system. Instead the young ruler was to give as the King requested. Also, the recourses were not to be given to the temple but to the poor. The rich young ruler declined. The command to sell all that he had may seem extreme, but tension between money, wealth and the King was immediately exposed. In this case, the man would not yield to the King of kings because he was submitted to another dominion and its currency.

After reassuring his disciples of the seemingly impossibility of rich people selling out for the Kingdom of God, Peter pointed out that, "we have left all we had to follow you!" Jesus responded "I tell you the truth, no one who has left home or wife or brothers or parents or children for the sake of the kingdom of God will fail to receive many times as much in this age and, in the age to

---

25 Matthew 16:16-17

come, eternal life."[26]

Paul said, I have lost all things for Christ[27] The disciples walked away from businesses, jobs and, for some, families for the King and His kingdom. Even their lives were forfeited for Him; and they considered it their joy to do so. They sold out completely to the King, not an idea, concept, organization, system of beliefs or a particular denomination. They sought the King and all these things were added unto them.[28]

Some may be asked to leave all to follow the King. Others may not be required to make that kind of sacrifice. In either case, the willingness of the individual to obey the King is what is tested. To whom much is given, much is required.[29] "If any man would come after Me, let him deny himself, take up his cross and follow Me."[30]

As Paul described the end of all things, he depicts a ceremony.

> Then the end will come, when he hands over the king-dom to God the Father after he has destroyed all do-minion, authority and power. For he must reign until he has put all his enemies under his feet. The last ene-my to be destroyed is death. For he "has put everything under his feet." Now when it says that "everything" has been put under him, it is clear that this does not in-clude God himself, who put everything under Christ. When he has done this, then the Son himself will be made subject to him who put everything under him, so that God may be all in all.[31]

God's order is restored. Those who rejected God's anointed King will begrudgingly confess that Jesus is Lord.[32] All who are connected to Christ serve as kings and priests around His throne. They share His nature, likeness and image. They sit with Him on His throne as sons and daughters. And they will reign with him

---

26 Luke 18:29-30
27 1 Corinthians 4:11-13, 16:18, 2 Corinthians 6:4-10
28 Matthew 6:33
29 See Luke 12:48
30 Matthew 16:24-26
31 1 Corinthians 15:24-28
32 Philippians 2:9-11

forever. That is the goal of the gospel of the Kingdom, and many have and will sell out completely when they find it.

Appendix

Suggested Reading

These are only a few of the many writers and their works that reinforced what the Spirit of God revealed in the scriptures. Use this brief list as a starting point to augment your study in the word.

Bevere, John
The Fear of the Lord Strang Communications: Lake Mary, FL 1997
Under Cover: Your Secret Place of Freedom Thomas Nelson: Nashville, TN 2001

Hagin, Kenneth
The Believer's Authority Faith Library Publications: Tulsa OK 2001

Hamon, Bill
Prophets and Personal Prophecy 1987, Prophets, Pitfalls and Principles 1990
Prophets and the Prophetic Movement 1991 Destiny Image: New Kensington, PA

Hayes, Norville
How to Live and Not Die Harrison House: Tulsa OK 2005

Jacobs, Cindy
The Voice of God Gospel Light: Ventura, CA 1997

Johnson, David, VanVonderen, Jeff
The Subtle Power of Spiritual Abuse 1991 Bethany House
Publishers Minneapolis, MN

Kline, Meredith G.
The Treaty of the Great King Eerdmans: Grand Rapids MI 1963

Munroe, Myles
The Power and Purpose of Praise and Worship 2000
The Power and Purpose of Prayer 2002
Understanding the Power and Purpose of Men 2001
Understanding the Power and Purpose of Women 2001 Destiny
Image: New Kensington, PA

Nee, Watchman
The Normal Christian Life Tyndale House: Wheaton, IL 1997
Sit, Stand, Walk 1997
The Breaking of the Outer Man 1997
Authority and Submission 1998
The Spiritual Man 1998
The Ministry of God's Word 2000
The Ministry of Christ 1997 Living Stream Ministry: Anaheim,
CA

Prince, Derek
Spiritual Warfare Whitaker House: New Kensington, PA 1987
They Shall Expel Demons Baker: Grand Rapids, MI 1998

Ratzlaff, Dale
The Sabbath in Christ Life Assurance Ministries: Glendale, CA
2003

Walters, S. Lloyd
The Father's Gift Scepter Communications: Altamonte Springs,
FL 2016

S. Lloyd Walters Bio

For over twenty years Pastor S. L. Walters has been involved in ministry as a practicing Pastor and Evangelist. His ministry has brought him to almost every major city on the East coast and elsewhere including:

Albany, NY	Fitzgerald, GA	Montgomery, AL
Hyde Park, NY	Orlando, FL	Shreveport, LA
Hempstead, NY	Flint, MI	Minden, LA
New York, NY	Berrien Springs, MI	Mansfield, LA
Boston, MA	Saint Joseph, MI	Metairie, LA
Springfield, MA	Benton Harbor, MI	Hammond, LA
Hartford, CT	Rochester, NY	New Orleans, LA
Bloomfield, CT	Winter Park, FL	Fort Worth, TX
New Haven, CT	Spartanburg, SC	Houston, TX
Newark, NJ	Pompano Beach, FL	Inglewood, CA
Philadelphia, PA	Fort Lauderdale, FL	Cassopolis, MI
Baltimore, MD	Dania, FL	Lansing, MI
Washington, DC	Hollywood, FL	Chicago, IL
Asheville, NC	Miami, FL	Grand Rapids, MI
Augusta, GA	Coconut Grove, FL	Brooklyn, NY
Atlanta, GA	Huntsville, AL	Staten Island, NY
Decatur, GA	Harvest, AL	
Tifton, GA	Birmingham, AL	

Pastor Walters has formal training in Religion and Broadcast Communications with BA and M.Div. Degrees. He has practical experience in broadcast media in the areas of:

Production Assistant   Technical Director
Camera Operator   Film Editor and Librarian
Film and Slide Chain Operator   Radio Announcer
Audio Engineer and Designer   Freelance Producer / Director

Now Pastor Walters' only focus is to teach, preach and promote the Gospel of the Kingdom of God and His Christ under the leadership and direction of the Spirit of God through the activities of Answer Ministries International Inc. and its affiliated ministries.

Made in the USA
Monee, IL
13 October 2023

44550156R00080